Transcendence in
Philosophy and Religion

Indiana Series in the Philosophy of Religion
Merold Westphal, general editor

Transcendence in Philosophy and Religion

Edited by
James E. Faulconer

INDIANA UNIVERSITY PRESS
BLOOMINGTON AND INDIANAPOLIS

This book is a publication of

Indiana University Press
601 North Morton Street
Bloomington, IN 47404-3797 USA

http://iupress.indiana.edu/~iupress

Telephone orders 800-842-6796
Fax orders 812-855-7931
Orders by e-mail iuporder@indiana.edu

The paper used in this publication meets the minimum require-
ments of American National Standard for Information Sciences—
Permanence of Paper for Printed Library Materials, ANSI
Z39.48-1984.

MANUFACTURED IN THE UNITED STATES OF AMERICA

Library of Congress Cataloging-in-Publication Data

Transcendence in philosophy and religion / edited by James E. Faulconer.
    p. cm.   — (Indiana series in the philosophy of religion)
Includes bibliographical references and index.
    ISBN 0-253-34199-X (alk. paper) — ISBN 0-253-21575-7 (pbk. : alk. paper)
1. Philosophy and religion. 2. Transcendence (Philosophy) 3. Hermeneutics.
I. Faulconer, James E. II. Series.
    B56 .T73 2003
    111'.6—dc21

                                                    2002012401

1 2 3 4 5 08 07 06 05 04 03

Contents

ACKNOWLEDGMENTS

My thanks to Brigham Young University for the leave during which I compiled these essays and to the many people, past and present, who have helped me with advice and criticism. I am especially grateful to my wife, Janice K. Faulconer, for her support and encouragement.

Transcendence in Philosophy and Religion

Introduction

Thinking Transcendence

James E. Faulconer

Since Kant, we have been faced with the question of how to think transcendence. Until the modern period, philosophy and religion were generally content to think transcendence without thinking the problematic of transcendence. Of course, the question of how to think the Divine was a perennial problem, but in a way quite different than it becomes with Hume and then Kant. The question was how to do so, not whether one could. However, with *Critique of Pure Reason*, all questions of transcendence are put outside the realm of objective thought. As Paul Ricoeur reminds us, that does not mean that rational theology comes to an end (*Le mal* 30). The work of theological thinkers deeply indebted to Kant, such as Fichte, Schelling, and Hegel, is evidence against any such claim, though the question to which they respond, "How are we to think transcendence or what is transcendent?" remains. A response to that question becomes the heart of any philosophical theology. But the question of transcendence is not relevant only to theology, philosophical or otherwise.

Though seldom noticed in the English speaking philosophical world, as Vincent Descombes has shown, from Alexandre Kojeve on, French philosophy has been concerned with the question of transcendence: How is it possible for there to be a relation to that which is, and remains, truly other? The work of thinkers like Emmanuel Levinas, on the one hand, and Jacques Derrida, on the other, has been taken up—though, in the Anglo-American world, more often by those in literature than in philosophy. But until recently few on this side of the Atlantic Ocean seem to have noticed that the question of transcendence is at the heart of that work. Perhaps it is not too much to suggest that the 1961 publication of Levinas's *Totality and Infinity* was especially important to making the question explicit. But *Totality and Infinity* is important not only because it makes the question of transcendence explicit but because, in doing so, it uses the language and concepts of religion, within philosophy, to talk about transcendence. Levinas explicitly wants to avoid confusing faith and philosophy.[1] Nevertheless, he does not hesitate to speak of God.[2] For Levinas, to speak of transcendence philosophically is to have what one says informed by an understanding with its roots in religion, even if that speaking is not itself religious.

After Levinas, others take a similar approach—thinkers such as Jean-François Courtine, Jean-Louis Chrétien, Michel Henry, Jean-Luc Marion, and (perhaps) Paul Ricoeur. Though the number of works produced by those thinkers is impressive, they have not been without their critics. In particular, there has been something like an ongoing discussion between Dominique Janicaud and those whom he criticizes, especially Marion and Henry, for whom Christianity offers an alternative way of thinking about phenomena.[3] Though both Marion and Henry deny that they are theologizing phenomenology,[4] Janicaud argues that what he calls "the theological turn" of French phenomenology—in other words, the turn toward the Other, the invisible, pure givenness, the Archi-Revelation, and so on—is a mistake and a departure from phenomenology to theology.[5] Like Levinas, some of those whom Janicaud criticizes are open about the fact that they see religion as offering new ways to think about the problem of transcendence in philosophy in its various manifestations. Nevertheless, they deny that they have ceased to do phenomenology or that they are doing theology. As the discussion between the two sides shows, the question of transcendence is alive and well in Paris.

There are a variety of ways of responding to the question of transcendence, but among those who believe that there are ways of doing so philosophically and not only theologically, there are two primary, related camps. One group can be said, roughly, to take a position similar to Ricoeur's: philosophy cannot decide whether the signs of religion point to some transcendent being, at least partly because philosophy is primarily an epistemological enterprise and religion is not.[6] But that does not mean that we cannot make a philosophical analysis of religious phenomena. Phenomenological analysis of religion is possible, but phenomenology is condemned "to run the gauntlet of a hermeneutic and precisely of a *textual* or *scriptural* hermeneutic" (Ricoeur, "Expérience" 130 [19]) in order to philosophize about religious things, including transcendence. Neither does the inability of philosophy to decide whether religion points to a transcendent being mean that religious thinking is irrelevant to or contradictory of philosophical and, specifically, phenomenological thought. The necessity of always beginning from a set of presuppositions means that the presuppositions of religion *may be* relevant to philosophical thought and that the analysis of religious phenomena may shed light on other phenomena.

The first two essays of this volume, those by Merold Westphal and Ben Vedder, both argue for the prereflective origin of all philosophical thought and the necessity of turning hermeneutically to prior interpretations, including religious ones, as a starting point for our philosophical reflections. The second two essays, by Paul Moyaert and James E. Faulconer, put into practice that which Westphal and Vedder argue for. They give us phenomenological reflections that start, respectively, from the Council of Trent and the biblical story of Moses and Israel. Together, these four essays represent one way that contemporary philosophy deals with the question of transcendence, something we might call a "hermeneutics of transcendence."

In "Whose Philosophy? Which Religion? Reflections on Reason as Faith," Westphal argues that religion and philosophy are the same in that both require faith. To be sure, philosophical faith and religious faith are not the same. But in spite of that difference, it is important to recognize that they share the general form of faith seeking understanding. Religion is faith seeking understanding; similarly, philosophy can be described as preunderstanding seeking elucidation. To recognize that both begin with a kind of faith is to recognize that there is no pure reason, that reason is shaped by the very thing from which it promises to free us—namely, our life-world. To demonstrate his claim, Westphal compares and contrasts the theodicies of Kant and Hegel to show their grounding in the philosophers' respective life worlds: "In the debate between Kant and Hegel and, perhaps, Augustine, we have a conflict of interpretations rather than the conquest of the Idea. Or, to put it a bit differently, we have different faiths seeking understanding" (21–22).

Against Janicaud's argument for a rigorous phenomenology and, so, for a phenomenology in which the "theological turn" is excluded, Westphal argues that the idea that philosophy should be a rigorous science has its origin in a life-world: "The life-world keeps showing up on the noesis side of the equation, insinuating itself into the transcendental ego, giving to it (and thus to philosophical reflection) a historically specific identity and depriving it of the naked neutrality that Husserl wanted it to retain" (26). The result is that philosophy is necessarily perspectival rather than a matter of intuition, and there is no a priori reason for excluding the life-world of religion from the life-world that gives us phenomenology. Westphal's argument takes us to the conclusion that religious experience may be relevant to phenomenological inquiry.

Vedder's essay, "The Question into Meaning and the Question of God: A

James E. Faulconer

Hermeneutic Approach," makes a related point differently. Since meaning requires context, Vedder argues, we understand the meaning of religious and philosophical claims about God and transcendence only if we understand the original narratives that motivate the issues that give rise to the claims in question. Stories of a religious tradition are the point of departure for religious thinking about God. Similarly, the question of the being and reality of God is understood within a prior narrative, a narrative that gives meaning to that question and its discussion. However, though both of these contexts use the same word, *God*, their discussions are not the same. In fact, the philosophical discussion is an outgrowth of the religious; it is one of several interpretations that can be given in response to the original stories.

Ideally, philosophical talk of God, what Vedder calls "transcendentology," and religious talk of God have a hermeneutic relation: transcendentology is linked to religion in apology; religious stories and experiences serve a corrective function for transcendentology. However, as Vedder says, "It may happen that the interpretation, although motivated by the initial issue, starts to lead a life of its own as the result of a pattern of thinking" (44), and this is what has happened in philosophy. The result is that philosophy has lost its way. When it comes to the matters of religion, "thinking is no longer calibrated to the original experience of meaning" (47). Philosophy and metaphysics must open the door and listen to what has already been said in religion, to what has made transcendentology possible.

In the first of two essays that take up this challenge to listen to what religion has said, "The Sense of Symbols as the Core of Religion: a Philosophical Approach to a Theological Debate," Moyaert asks what it is that makes a person open and receptive to religion: what is the human foundation for religion? He answers, "A sense for symbols." Moyaert takes up the discussion of the Eucharist at the Council of Trent to make his case, and he uses his analysis to give new understanding to the decision at Trent in favor of transubstantiation. Moyaert argues that sacramental acts make up the core of Christian faith, with the Eucharist at the center of those acts. On this view, transcendence is not something merely other-worldly, for "despite his transcendence, God is *really present* in the sacramental acts carried out in his name" (56). Thus, transcendence is to be understood by examining orthopraxy rather than orthodoxy, for the confession of belief is itself "a ritualized, elemental component of orthopraxy" (56).

Relying on Michael Polanyi's distinction between signs and symbols, as well as his own analysis of symbolic phenomena, Moyaert points out that symbols can have the meaning of intimate contact. One need not recollect that to which the symbol points for the symbol to do its work. One need only reverence the symbol. But this underscores the claim that praxis, not dogma, is at the heart of the symbolic and of transcendence. As a result, Moyaert argues, by insisting on the doctrine of transubstantiation, the Council of Trent was trying to rescue the understanding of the Eucharist from rational theology, making theology a *theologia orans* instead. This means, Moyaert argues, that, if religion is relevant to thinking transcendence philosophically, we will find that relevance in *theologia orans* rather than in rational theology.

The second essay to attempt to find a touchstone of phenomenological possibilities in religion is Faulconer's "Philosophy and Transcendence: Religion and the Possibility of Justice." For Faulconer, the proximate issue is justice rather than the Eucharist, and his source is the Bible rather than a Church Council. Nevertheless, his interest is the same: How does religion think transcendence and what might that suggest about how philosophy can think it? The problem of justice is straightforward: We must go beyond our own contexts and histories if we are to be just, but there is no acontextual and ahistorical vantage point from which to do so. Though we often invoke the Golden Rule as a guide to justice, that rule requires that there be reciprocity between myself and the other person when the possibility of reciprocity may be the very thing in question.

Using an analysis of the biblical story of Moses and Israel, Faulconer recognizes that there can be no question that this story establishes Israel and, therefore, the possibility of justice by appealing to transcendence. Nevertheless, the transcendence in question is not merely that of something radically outside of this world. He argues that the biblical story shows us two kinds of transcendence, historical transcendence—we always have both a past and a future that is not of our making but that constitutes us—and a transcendence in which historical transcendence is, itself, always interrupted and requires constant recuperation. We find ourselves in a context that is both determinate and indeterminate. Thus, "Biblical religion suggests that we look for transcendence not by looking beyond this world, but by looking within this world for that which calls us to justice by breaking or interrupting our understanding of justice" (82).

The last three essays of this volume, under the heading "Rethinking Phenomenology," differ from the first four. Rather than looking to religious practices and texts as the source for thinking transcendence, the essays confront the issue of transcendence directly, though only one of them, Marion's, argues that such a direct approach can be successful. The direct approach is the second approach to transcendence, one that we see in the work of Marion as well as in the writing of Michel Henry. It would be a mistake to think that there is a sharp dichotomy between the work of those such as Marion and Henry and the understanding that we see in the work of those such as Ricoeur, Westphal, Vedder, Moyaert, and Faulconer. As Westphal's and Vedder's references to Marion show, there is overlap between the hermeneutical phenomenology of the kind that Westphal and Vedder argue for and the approach that Marion takes. Nevertheless, Marion does not believe that phenomenology can turn only to hermeneutics in order to deal with transcendence, and on that point there is considerable disagreement. For Marion, it is possible to deal with the pure phenomenon of revelation and, therefore, transcendence, and it is possible to do so philosophically and not only theologically. That claim is the issue of the second group of essays.

In "The Event, the Phenomenon, and the Revealed," Marion argues that givenness precedes manifestation; therefore, we must look to manifestation to see, indirectly, whether we can find some trace of the givenness of things, of donation. Marion uses the hall at the Catholic Institute of Paris where the paper was delivered, the *Salle des Actes*, to show the trace of donation in the phenomenon. He points out that any full description of the event would be infinitely long. However, if that is the case, then the event of the lecture hall cannot be a merely constituted object. It is also a given. That is the heart of Marion's argument, a heart that he defends against objections, most notably those that focus on the objective and atemporal character of the event. For example, one can ask, "If the event of the hall is marked by its givenness, how is it that one can miss the phenomenality of the hall by reducing it to objectivity?" Following Kant, Marion's answer is that the foreseeable quality of the hall "turns it into an object . . . as if there were nothing else to be seen in it . . . than what can already be envisaged on the basis of its construction plan" (91). In fact, when we are dealing with technical objects, it is enough to foresee them and not to see them. Seeing technical objects will only get in the way of their function as technical objects. Thus, in such a view, the event in which the thing was given has always already disappeared. Nothing unexpected can show itself in such objects. For Marion, the analysis of the happening of events shows us that in every case what shows itself can only do so in virtue of "a strictly and eidetically phenomenological *self* [which is not an *ego*], which guarantees only that it gives *itself* and that, in return, it proves that its phenomenalization presupposes its givenness as such and from itself" (93). In the case of my birth, Marion argues, we have a phenomenon that gives itself without showing itself, a giving without manifestation. "The origin, which refuses to show itself, does not, however, *give itself* through poverty (Derrida), but through excess" (97); it gives itself before it shows itself.

An important implication of this analysis is that, in giving itself, the phenomenon "confiscates the function and the role of the self in the process, thus conceding to the ego only a secondary and derived *me*" (98). The transcendental ego does not have a transcendental function and is not the ultimate foundation of the experience of phenomena; the ego no longer has any transcendental claim. It is neither active nor passive, but receptive: passively active. It is the "given-to" (*l'adonné*). The given-to receives the given, fixing it, bringing its phenomenalizing to a halt. In doing so, it makes both the given and itself visible. This fixing is a matter of its resistance to the given; the resistance of the given-to transmutes the excess of phenomenality into visibility and, in doing so, also shows the excessiveness of phenomenality.

Marion argues that this breakdown of the gap between the given and the phenomenal is also a breakdown of the gap between the objects of rational thought and the objects of revelation. The consequence is that "the givens retrieved by Revelation—in this instance, the unique Jewish and Christian Revelation—must be read and treated as legitimate phenomena, subject to the same operations as those that result from the givens of the world" (104).

In "Phenomenality and Transcendence," Marlène Zarader takes up Marion's rethinking of phenomenology and Janicaud's challenge to that rethinking by asking whether one can affirm transcendence within phenomenology. Heidegger, she says, has set up the problem of transcendence by saying that, on the one hand, philosophy can have nothing to do with what absents itself absolutely and, on the other hand, some realities withdraw from all presence. Having set up the problem in that way, Heidegger deplored "philosophy's inability to envision a radical alterity" (107) and appealed to the necessity of renewing thought, motions repeated in Levinas and Marion. For these thinkers, the question is how these limits of philosophy apply to phenomenology. As they see it, Husserl's phenomenology may reproduce the metaphysical determination of presence and, so, the limits of philosophy, but that does not mean that another phenomenology is not possible, one that would do justice to givenness and, so, to transcendence. Both Levinas and Marion offer alternatives to Husserlian phenomenology, and they do so by seeking the mark of the transcendent in phenomena themselves.

On the face of it, this seems to imply a contradiction: The transcendent must preserve its alterity, placing it beyond what phenomenology has heretofore understood as the conditions of possible experience, while, at the same time, transcendence must be inscribed in an experience. Following the strategy laid out by Heidegger, both Levinas and Marion deal with this seeming contradiction by arguing that I do not lay hold of the transcendent. It lays hold of me. In Marion, this takes the form of a witness struck by powerlessness in "the counter-experience of a non-object" (112). However, Zarader wants to know whether such a *pure* experience, an experience of pure powerlessness, is possible, and she argues, with Janicaud, that it is not. It is possible to think an experience with no object, but not an experience with no subject and, so, not a pure experience: "By insisting on the powerlessness of the witness, [Marion] seems to deprive the witness of all the powers of the subject; but since he grants the witness the function of 'filter' of phenomena (a filter meant to assure the possibility of their manifestation), he reestablishes, without admitting it, what he claims to have dismissed" (115). Thus, argues Zarader, Levinas and Marion go too far not by arguing that the Other exceeds the form of the object, but by radically removing all constitution from the experience of the Other: "If thought wishes to embrace anything, even a nothing, it necessarily presupposes a *there* that guarantees the meaning of the being of this nothing, thus causing it to escape from *pure* alterity" (116). It does not follow that thought must renounce the possibility of accord with anything beyond the circle of immanence. One can think transcendence *in* immanence as the perturbation or subversion of the order of phenomena.

Béatrice Han's contribution, "Transcendence and the Hermeneutic Circle: Some Thoughts on Marion and Heidegger," is also critical of Marion's attempt to think transcendence directly, but, relying on Marion's early work, she finds the project interesting for the criticism that it makes of Heidegger: According to Marion, in Heidegger "the ontological anteriority of being over any ontic manifestation excludes the possibility of *anything* showing up that would distort or exceed the space of disclosure thus opened" (122). The implications of this criticism are relevant not only to thinking about divine transcendence, but to the more general case of thinking about anything outside the hermeneutical circle. However, Han argues, Marion's reading of Heidegger is incomplete and often faulty. In sum, the problem is that Marion takes a Heideggerian stance but makes criticisms of Heidegger that can make sense only from a non-Heideggerian standpoint. In addition, she argues, Marion's own position is invalid because its premises assume a phenomenological understanding of transcendence while its conclusion reverts to the metaphysical concept of transcendence. However, says Han, these kinds of difficulties are typical of those who try to step outside of the hermeneutic circle rather than to remain within its limits and relate to those limits differently.

Han begins with a summary of Marion's argument in *God Without Being*. According to Marion, the divine is fully disclosed in the idol, without opacity or residue, but it cannot exceed the limits of that disclosure. The fullness of disclosure in the idol is a mark of the fact that it is constituted by the human gaze. In contrast, the icon discloses the impossibility of a full disclosure of the divine. The icon "shows the limits of phenomenality itself by exceeding our powers of representation" (124). For Marion, Heidegger's understanding of God is idolatrous rather than iconic, so it must determine God in advance as a being. Marion's solution to the problem is to argue that what is disclosed, the transcendent, must open up the space of its own disclosure, which means that space will be incommensurable to any human faculties. This argument against Heidegger is flawed by three fundamental errors: it reads Heidegger from a Husserlian—in other words, extrinsic—point of view; it makes our understanding of being dependent on *Dasein*; and it unduly narrows Heidegger's understanding of phenomenality. The last of these is perhaps the most devastating of these criticisms, for, Han argues, it means that, contrary to Marion's reading of Heidegger, not everything that is disclosed must be disclosed as a being nor disclosed by *Dasein*. As Heidegger makes clear in writings such as "The Origin of the Work of Art," there are entities that reveal themselves without that revelation being dependent on *Dasein* for its constitution. Such revelations show that the hermeneutic circle was never as closed as Marion takes it to be. In fact, they show that Heidegger's understanding of disclosure is iconic rather than idolatrous. Before Marion, Heidegger understands thinking as receptivity, which is not simply passivity and clearly not merely activity.

However, Marion's answer to the problem of the hermeneutic circle is different than is Heidegger's. Han reconstructs Marion's argument syllogistically (136):

a) "The question of being is only relevant from the perspective of the relationship between being and *Dasein*, and within this context determines the meaning of the world."

b) "God does not belong to this world."

Therefore c), "the question of being, which is relevant only to *Dasein* and the world, does not apply to God: God is beyond being."

The argument is, however, unsound: Setting aside the problem of the second premise—the problem of how one would establish its truth—Han argues that the first premise confuses the conditions of existence and the conditions of phenomenal manifestation.

Han's final criticism is similar to Zarader's: Marion's idea that one can think God without condition is a logical impossibility. In arguing for such a possibility, Marion is reverting to a metaphysical understanding of transcendence; he uncritically takes up a pre-Kantian understanding of transcendence in which the thing itself is unconditionally disclosive.

In spite of the fact that Han thinks that Marion's criticism of Heidegger is untenable and that his own answer to the problem of transcendence is self-contradictory, she also finds his work interesting. It brings the question of the limits of phenomenological disclosure into the foreground. Though Marion fails, "this failure is valuable in that it shows us that the danger of hermeneutic closure cannot be dealt with by means of a sheer denial of the hermeneutic circle itself" (138).

The common thread in these essays is the need to think what is outside the hermeneutic circle. All but Marion think that it can be done only hermeneutically—in other words, from within the circle. They argue that there is no pure revelation of what is outside to we who stand inside: no revelation of the Other can be dissociated from the horizon into which that revelation projects itself. Thus, the question that remains is whether a revelation of transcendence can be pure or whether the pure revelation of transcendence, when fixed by the receiver, can remain pure. If the answer is yes, then the textual detour required by a hermeneutical phenomenology of transcendence is not the only possibility for speaking philosophically of transcendence. However, if the answer is no, then hermeneutics seems to be the only option, though, as these essays suggest, it will be a broken hermeneutics, a hermeneutics that operates in the traces of rupture and subversion.

NOTES

1. See, for example, *Éthique et infini* (14–15 [24–25]) and *Of God Who Comes to Mind* (85–86). Throughout, page numbers in brackets refer to the page numbers of the respective translation.

2. Perhaps the best place to see his use of God in summary is in "God and Philosophy" (*Comes to Mind* 55–78).

3. I say "something like" because, though Janicaud has criticized Levinas, Marion,

Henry, and others directly, their response has not been direct. See Courtine, *Phénoménologie et théologie*.

4. It is clear from such pieces as "Phénomène saturé" and "The Event" (the latter in this volume) that Marion believes that religious phenomena raise issues that are relevant to phenomena in general (*Phénomène* 80 [176–177]). See Henry for a similar position (*C'est moi* 7).

5. See Janicaud, *Le tournant théologique* and *La phénoménologie éclatée*. See also the responses to the first of these by Courtine, Chrétien, Henry, Marion, and Ricoeur in *Phénomenologie et théologie*.

6. Ricoeur makes this argument in a number of places. See, for example, *The Symbolism of Evil*.

WORKS CITED

Courtine, Jean-François, ed. *Phénoménologie et théologie*. Paris: Criterion, 1992. Translated in Dominique Janicaud et al., *Phenomenology and the "Theological Turn": The French Debate*, trans. Bernard G. Prusak, Jeffrey L. Kosky, and Thomas A. Carlson, 104–241. New York: Fordham University Press, 2000.

Henry, Michel. *C'est moi, la verité*. Paris: Seuil, 1996.

Janicaud, Dominique. *La phénoménologie éclatée*. Paris: L'Éclat, 1998.

———. *La tournant théologique de la phénoménologie française*. Paris: L'Éclat, 1991. Translated in Dominique Janicaud et al., *Phenomenology and the "Theological Turn": The French Debate*, trans. Bernard G. Prusak, Jeffrey L. Kosky, and Thomas A. Carlson, 16–103. New York: Fordham University Press, 2000.

Janicaud, Dominique, Jean-François Courtine, Jean-Louis Chrétien, Jean-Luc Marion, Michel Henry, and Paul Ricoeur. *Phenomenology and the "Theological Turn": The French Debate*. Trans. Bernard G. Prusak, Jeffrey L. Kosky, and Thomas A. Carlson. New York: Fordham University Press, 2000.

Levinas, Immanuel. *De Dieu qui vient à l'idée*. Paris: Librairie Philosophique, 1986. Translated as *Of God Who Comes to Mind*. Trans. Bettina Bergo. Stanford, Calif.: Stanford University Press, 1986.

———. *Totalité et infini*. The Hague: Nijhoff, 1961. Translated as *Totality and Infinity*. Trans. Alphonso Lingis. Pittsburgh: Duquesne University Press, 1969.

Marion, Jean-Luc. "Le phénomène saturé." In Jean-François Courtine, ed., *Phénoménologie et théologie*, 79–127. Paris: Criterion, 1991. Translated as "The Saturated Phenomenon," in Dominique Janicaud et al., *Phenomenology and the "Theological Turn": The French Debate*, trans. Bernard G. Prusak, Jeffrey L. Kosky, and Thomas A. Carlson, 176–216. New York: Fordham University Press, 2000.

Ricoeur, Paul. "Expérience et langage dans le discours religieux." In *Phénoménologie et théologie*, ed. Jean-François Courtine, 15–39. Paris: Criterion, 1991. Translated as "Experience and Language in Religious Discourse," in Dominique Janicaud et al., *Phenomenology and the "Theological Turn": The French Debate*, trans. Bernard G. Prusak, Jeffrey L. Kosky, and Thomas A. Carlson, 127–146. New York: Fordham University Press, 2000.

———. *Le mal. Un défi à la philosophie et à la théologie*. Geneva: Labor et Fides, 1996.

———. *The Symbolism of Evil*. Trans. Emerson Buchanan. New York: Harper & Row, 1967.

PART I. HERMENEUTICS AND PHILOSOPHICAL REFLECTION

Whose Philosophy?
Which Religion?

Reflections on Reason as Faith

Merold Westphal

Credo ut intelligam

—Augustine

Fides quaerens intellectum

—Anselm

Metaphysics is the finding of bad reasons for what we believe upon instinct.

—F. H. Bradley

At the beginning of his Fourth Critique, Kant insists both that "morality does not need religion at all [*keinesweges*]" and that it "leads ineluctably [*unumgänglich*] to religion" (*Religion* 3 and 5). In this *keinesweges* and *unumgänglich* we have Kant's adverbial definition of the best of all possible worlds. We can have our cake and eat it too. We can be religious without sacrificing autonomy. At one level, this has nothing at all to do with philosophy. Kant is emphatic that "neither science nor philosophy is needed in order to know what one must do to be honest and good" and that the idea of the good will "already dwells in the natural sound understanding and needs not so much to be taught as merely elucidated" (*Grounding* 16 and 9). But the point of departure for his version of rational religion is his own moral philosophy, not moral common sense, so we can read him as also saying that moral philosophy does not need religion but leads ineluctably thereto.

Kant says almost the same thing about theoretical philosophy when he prefaces the second edition of his first *Critique* by saying that he has "found it necessary to deny *knowledge* in order to make room for *faith*" by presenting a philosophy in which "all objections to morality and religion will be forever silenced." The *assumption* of God, freedom, and immortality becomes permissible only when "speculative reason [is] deprived of its pretensions to transcendent insight" (*Pure Reason* B xxx–xxxi). To use a metaphor from American football, theoretical reason is the blocking back that knocks down the opposing linebackers, while practical reason carries the ball into the end zone for the touchdown. "It was a team effort," as they say in the postgame locker-room interviews.

So it is not just moral philosophy, but philosophy as such, as the teamwork of theoretical and practical reason, of which Kant can say, it has no need of religion at all but leads ineluctably thereto.

Is he right about this? Does philosophy lead to religion?

I will lay my cards on the table at once by answering with two questions of my own: Whose philosophy? Which religion?

Usually when someone answers a question with a question, to say nothing of answering one with two, the purpose is to deflect the initial question, to avoid an unwelcome inquiry by putting the questioner in question. It is a defensive reaction guided by the maxim that the best defense is a good offense. When my team is about to put the ball into the net or into the end zone, the other team's chances of scoring are virtually nil.

In this case, however, I am eager to reply to the question, especially at a time when the notion that "reason" signifies a universal, secular neutrality is increasingly seen as a dubious dogma. These days, a healthy skepticism greets both the notion that thought can occupy the "view from nowhere" and the more specific claim that this is done by leaving God and religion out of the picture. No doubt there are delimited areas where such notions make sense, and we can be glad that there are few enthusiasts for Catholic chemistry or Methodist microbiology. But the attempt to force the whole life of the mind into this Procrustean bed, which we might call the rape of reason, is increasingly discredited, though it is not by any means dead.

It is not to avoid the question of whether philosophy leads to religion that I respond with my own questions, Whose philosophy? Which religion? It is, rather, to remind us that neither philosophy nor religion is one thing. But it is also to suggest that in all its varieties, and not just in the Augustinian/Christian versions, philosophy is faith seeking understanding. Or vision seeking articulation.

The faith of which I speak here is not necessarily religious faith, even in the broadest sense of the term, nor does it occur only in the context of religious reflection. It is, rather, the presuppositions with which philosophical reflection begins, on which it depends and from which it cannot free itself in any wholesale sense. These are the preunderstandings of Heidegger, the prejudices of Gadamer, the beliefs by virtue of which we find ourselves in the hermeneutical circle where reflection can begin. Just as human artisans do not create *ex nihilo* but make something out of something, so human thought is not the "Let there be light" that brings something out of nothing but the movement from somewhere to somewhere else. To speak of the somewhere where thought begins as faith is to remind ourselves of two senses in which thought's presuppositions are not the products of rational reflection.

We can begin with the Wittgensteinian/Foucauldian sense. We bring prephilosophical beliefs with us to philosophical reflection. These beliefs, which fall along the spectrum from tacit to fully explicit, are tightly wedded to forms of life or practices in two ways. On the one hand, they arise out of the language games in which we become competent players. We come to hold them primarily by being socialized into the life of a human community;[1] on the other hand, these beliefs shape both our attitudes and our actions. In this way, they serve to reinforce and legitimize the life-worlds which are their bearers.

Such beliefs are part of our identity, and we can speak of them as commitments, though, of course, they may be shallow and ephemeral commitments. They represent the "opinions," "traditions," and "sedimentations" from which philosophy has tried so valiantly to extricate itself in order to be pure reason—but in vain. Thus, to speak of philosophy as faith seeking understanding is to recognize (negatively) that we can neutralize these prereflective beliefs and the practices in which they are embedded *keinesweges,* and (positively) that they insinuate themselves into our most sophisticated reflection *unumgänglich.* Human thought is always situated. Reason is never pure.

There is also a Plantingian sense in which philosophy presupposes beliefs that are not the products of rational reflection. Plantinga is a soft foundationalist.[2] He holds that while some of our beliefs depend evidentially upon other beliefs, some do not. These latter, "basic" beliefs may be grounded in experience of some sort, such as sense perception, but that is not the same as having other beliefs (or the propositions expressing them) as their evidential basis. To know that the rose I am looking at is red, I need experience but not evidence. In believing that the rose that appears to me to be red really is red, I may also believe that I am not color-blind. But I do not believe the rose to be red *on the basis* of my belief that my vision is functioning properly.

Classical (or hard) foundationalism seeks to erect the edifice of knowledge on a *fundamentum inconcussum* by restricting the domain of properly basic beliefs to those with an objective certainty (no mere subjective certitude) stemming from self-evidence or incorrigibility. Knowledge is built on knowledge. Faith plays no part.

While affirming soft foundationalism, Plantinga rejects the classical version as a pipe dream motivated by unwarranted evidentialist assumptions about warrant. This leaves us with belief systems which include at their foundations beliefs that are not the products of rational reflection, which are not accepted "on the basis of argument or inference or demonstration" ("Reason" 158). It is quite natural to say that such beliefs are products of faith rather than reason. But such an analysis gives no support to fideism, if by that term is meant something like what Peirce calls the "method of tenacity." If someone points to (apparent) facts that (seem to) suggest that I am color-blind, I cannot appeal to Plantinga and respond that my beliefs are properly basic and thus immune to critical evaluation.[3]

We must notice two things about the belief systems described in this way. First, they are not necessarily religious in content. Among the beliefs that will stem from faith rather than reason *in this sense* are the belief in the reality of the external world, the belief in the reality of other minds, the belief that the past extends back further than five minutes, and the belief that the future will be like the past in the sense required by inductive inference. (What is distinctive about these particular beliefs is that philosophers, after long and futile effort, have become increasingly convinced that there are no noncircular proofs of them to be found.)

Second, and for our purposes more important, some of the belief systems that will have this structure will have the form of explicitly articulated theories, including philosophical theories. To say that philosophy is faith seeking understanding is to say not just 1) that prereflective beliefs, often more nearly tacit than explicit and deeply embedded in practices, play an ineliminable role in philosophical reflection, behind our back, as it were, but also 2) that basic beliefs take up visible residence within our theories without the benefit of propositional evidence, devoid of the imprimatur of "argument or inference or demonstration." An example of this second case, to which I shall return, is the belief that philosophy should and can be presuppositionless, rigorous science.

Closely related to the idea that philosophy is faith seeking understanding, whether that faith has a religious content or not, is the notion that philosophy is vision seeking articulation. Who can doubt that the powerful hold of Plato's *Republic* on subsequent European thought or of Spinoza's *Ethics* on German thought during the *Goethezeit* stems more from a bold and captivating picture of things than from cogent, irrefutable argumentation. Postmodernism attempts to rehabilitate rhetoric vis-à-vis logic, and Richard Rorty claims, more specifically, that it is in literature rather than philosophy that we think through our deepest moral and existential questions. Postmodernism and Rorty remind us that pictures and stories have a power over our thinking that analysis and argument at times can only envy.

Philosophers, however reluctant to acknowledge this fact, are not blind to it. They paint pictures, invent images, and tell tales (sometimes tall tales that can be called metanarratives) in the effort to persuade their readers. Even when they would like to think that their rhetoric is in the service of their logic, a closer look will often reveal that their arguments derive from and are in the service of a *Welt-bild* or *Weltanschauung* (which, in turn, as Wittgenstein and Foucault are eager to remind us, are embedded in some *Welt-Praxis*) more than vice versa. Here the notion that reason is never pure becomes the notion that philosophy is not capable of immaculate conception. Its most pregnant ideas are always already impregnated by symbols and stories that inform reason—that is, give it the DNA by which it will be shaped. The irony is that the "pure" reason which, according to a certain philosophical myth, sets out to enact the triumph of *logos* over *mythos*, of *noesis* and *episteme* over *eikasia* and *pistis* and *doxa*, is itself shaped by and in the service of that from which it promises to free us.

The notions of philosophy as faith seeking understanding and as vision seeking articulation give a certain specificity to the notion that neither philosophy nor reason is one thing. Some philosophies lead to religion; others do not. Those that do, do so in many different ways. There are many varieties of religion within the limits of reason alone, and quite a few different ways of insisting that religion should not be put in such a straitjacket. Hence the questions: Whose philosophy? Which religion? The preceding analysis provides us with helpful tools for analyzing these differences. We can ask:

1. *What is the life-world* out of which this philosophy emerges, and which of the former's commitments have shaped the latter most decisively?

2. *What are the basic beliefs* of this philosophy, the ones that serve as its "axioms" or "definitions" or "control beliefs" (see Wolterstorff) or "inference tickets" (see Ryle)?

3. What is the *Weltanschauung*, or metanarrative, which is the whole to which these basic beliefs belong in a hermeneutical circle of part and whole?

These questions signify the profound truth in the notion that "metaphysics is the finding of bad reasons for what we believe upon instinct," however irreverent and hyperbolic that formulation of *fides quaerens intellectum* may be. To the degree that we can answer these questions, we will better understand why certain philosophies do not lead to religion and, more important for the present discussion, why certain philosophies lead to the particular religions that they do. The "particular religion" in any given case might be some "organized" religion already on the scene as a more or less widely shared language game to which the philosopher relates more or less closely. But it need not be. It could just as well be a free-standing philosophical construct, such as, for example, Nietzsche's Dionysian/Zarathustrian religion.

Before analyzing three philosophies and the religions to which they lead, I want to introduce a further element crucial for understanding the relation of philosophy and religion. Philosophy not only leads to religion, but often serves to critique religion. Thus, even before the first *Critique* makes room for faith, in the preface to the second edition, it announces the critique of religion in the preface to the first edition. In a familiar footnote we read,

> Our age is, in especial degree, the age of criticism, and to criticism *every-thing* must submit. Religion through its sanctity, and law-giving through its majesty, may seek to exempt themselves from it. But then they awaken just suspicion, and cannot claim the sincere respect which reason accords only to what which has been able to sustain the test of free and open examination. (A xxii; emphasis added)[4]

We hear something quite similar when Heidegger discusses the relation of philosophy as phenomenological ontology to theology as an ontic, positive science that is *"absolutely different from philosophy . . .* closer to chemistry and mathematics than to philosophy" ("Phenomenology" 6).[5] Sounding very much like Johannes Climacus in Kierkegaard's *Philosophical Fragments*, Heidegger emphasizes the dependence of Christian theology on revelation and faith as rebirth, eventually concluding that it is a "fully autonomous ontic science" vis-à-vis philosophy (9–12, 16).[6] Immediately, however, he takes this back: "If faith does not need philosophy, the *science* of faith as a *positive* science does" (17). Like every ontic science, theology "operates within the basic context of an ontology, firstly and for the most part hidden" (17). The clarification and explication of the ontological dimension of science is the task of phenomenology. In part, this is because philosophy is the ontological science, by contrast with all the ontic sciences. But there is another reason. Faith is the *Aufhebung* of "pre-faith-full, i.e., unbelieving, human existence" (18). For this reason alone, "all basic theological concepts . . . have as their *ontological* determinants meanings which are pre-Christian and which can thus be grasped rationally" (18).

In keeping with the notion of formal indication that he developed in the period before *Being and Time*,[7] Heidegger emphasizes the formal character of ontological explication. But now he sounds more like Hegel than like Kierkegaard. Philosophy possesses a purely rational, formal knowledge that theology "needs"—for guidance, for codirection, and, nine times in two pages, for correction ("Phenomenology" 19–20).

There are philosophies that do not lead to religion but only critique it, though these may be fewer than they seem. We need only to think of Nietzsche's religion, already mentioned, the religion which Bertrand Russell calls "a free man's worship,"[8] and Marx's 1843 claim that the criticism of religion "ends with the doctrine that man is the highest being for man" (69). Of more interest presently is the fact that philosophies that do lead to religion lead not only to some particular religion, but in the process inevitably and, for the most part, not just implicitly critique other particular religions or types of religion. So the question of how and in what ways philosophy leads to religion has as its flip side the question of how and in what ways philosophy criticizes religion. The defense attorney in one case is the prosecuting attorney in another.

***

Kant's philosophy leads to religion. So does Hegel's. But, while both purport to be religion within the limits of reason alone, the religions to which they lead are far more different from each other than is Protestantism from Catholicism or Judaism, Christianity, and Islam from each other. Let us explore this difference in terms of our three questions: about the life-world horizons of their thought, about the basic beliefs within each system, and about the symbols and stories which make up the big picture that stands in a mutually constitutive relation with the parts of the system.

That human reason should and can be autonomous is a basic belief shared by Kant and Hegel. This belief arises out of the life-world of a cultural elite roughly identified as the Enlightenment, into which both Kant and Hegel were socialized; and it belongs to the grand narrative of the Enlightenment about "the emancipation of the rational subject" (Lyotard xxiii). In general, it means that reason can and should be pure, *episteme* uncontaminated by *doxa*.

There are two theological corollaries to this belief. First, essential, proper religious knowledge cannot be dependent on faith as the reception of divine revelation in the traditional senses of these terms, namely, that we need to know what we cannot discover with the resources of unaided human reason, that God gives us what we cannot provide for ourselves, and that faith is (in part) the trusting reception of this gift.[9] This gift, this epistemic grace, is not compatible with the self-sufficiency of human reason signified by the autonomy claim.

Second, historical narratives cannot, as such, be essential to the content of religious knowledge, for 1) reason cannot generate anything historically specific from itself, and 2) if it is to remain autonomous, it can be expected only to recognize universal, essential truths in historical narratives. Thus, for Kant, such narratives can serve as "examples" or "vehicles" of what pure practical reason knows without their help. Like the diagrams that Socrates draws for the slave boy, narratives can be pedagogically useful but not philosophically ultimate. It is not necessary to quarrel over the historicity of such narratives, for if we think of them as parables or myths they can do their job just as well. For example, in the stories of Jesus,[10] we are dealing with *"The Personified Idea of the Good Principle. . . .* We need, therefore, no empirical example to make the idea of a person morally well-pleasing to God our archetype; this idea as an archetype is already present in our reason . . . [and] is to be sought nowhere but in our own reason" (*Religion* 54, 56–57). Of course, Kant does not deny the existence of Jesus, but Jesus' existence is no more necessary to the proper moral use of his story than is that of the Good Samaritan.

Being more historically oriented, Hegel treats the actual existence of Jesus as theologically important, but only because of its role in triggering a *Wesens-schau*, in helping us to see that the human and divine natures are one, not uniquely in Jesus but universally. It is this universal truth that is the proper content of theology, and Jesus helps us to recollect it. To return to the "slave boy" analogy, the diagrams are now necessary to the recollection, by Hegel's account, but the truth recollected is not about them. The doctrine of the Incarnation is not about Jesus but about the relation of two essences, human nature and divine nature. The content of theology, as it is for Kant, is universal truth; historical particularity as such remains scandalous. It is clear 1) that the religions to which the philosophies of Kant and Hegel will lead will not be any version of orthodox Christianity, Eastern or Western, Catholic or Protestant, and 2) that their philosophies will be critiques, sometimes very sharp, of all such theologies for refusing to stay within the limits of reason alone.

Beyond this common ground, it is necessary to speak of the religions—plural—to which the philosophies of Kant and Hegel lead, because they are very different indeed. On the one hand, Kant finds radical evil in human nature, not moral weakness but the free choice of an overriding evil maxim which permits the triumph of inclination over duty whenever the costs of doing one's duty get too high or, to say essentially the same thing, whenever the benefits of following inclination get high enough to "warrant" the substitution of *prudent* for *wrong*.

By contrast, and in keeping with his affirmation of the essential divinity of human nature, Hegel finds an innocence that would almost make Nietzsche happy and that permits Kierkegaard's Climacus to say that the system has no ethics (*Postscript* 119, 121, 145, 307, 327, 346). The Fall is inseparable from the Creation and turns out to be a fall upwards, from animal immediacy to human mediation, the awareness of a cognitive lack, the need for truth. "Humanity ought not to be innocent" (Hegel 3:298).[11] To say that humanity is by nature evil is to speak not of fault but of finitude, and cognitive finitude at that. It is to say that at the outset we have not yet achieved our cognitive destiny, absolute knowledge.

We have before us the following awkward situation: out of one side of its mouth, presumably pure reason says that there is radical evil in the human will, while out of the other side of its mouth it tells a totally different story. We are forced to ask, when reason makes these announcements, whose reason is speaking? Kant's *drama* is dramatically different from Hegel's.

If we are led to suspect that neither is the voice of pure reason, we can ask about the life-worlds out of which these basic beliefs about human nature arise. In the case of Kant we cannot doubt the lasting impact of the Pietism to which he was exposed in his youth, both at home and at school. The pure practical reason of the mature Kant was never so pure as to be beyond the shaping influence of this Christian life-world, however hostile he was to the church's doctrines and rites. Hegel, at least during his gymnasium and seminary days, was exposed to a Christianity more toward the rationalist than the Pietist end of the spectrum. Even more decisive, it would appear, is a later phase of his formation, his socialization into a community of three (with Schelling and Hölderlin, after their years together at Tübingen Seminary) for whom the idealism of Fichte's 1794 *Wissenschaftslehre* provided the framework for a decisive break with theism through its essentially Spinozistic character.[12] Such a community easily—one is tempted to say automatically—becomes Gnostic in its religion, taking the highest human task to be speculation rather than the rectification of the individual's perverse will.

Corresponding to these very different life-worlds inhabited by Kant and Hegel at decisive stages in their formation are two very different metanarratives, containing the Pelagian and Gnostic soteriologies, respectively. For Kant, the Enlightenment myth of progress is not only the grand story of the emancipation of the rational subject, but also the eschatological narrative of the building of *ein ethisches gemeines Wesen*, the invisible church of those striving for moral perfection without the "benefit" of creeds or rituals or the clergy who accompany them, and with only such divine assistance as they merit after having converted themselves, not to God but to the Good Principle.

By contrast, Hegel's eschatology is the speculative metanarrative, as Lyotard has labeled it, the logical, phenomenological, and ultimately historical story of the emergence and triumph of Science: Absolute Knowing. This knowledge is the highest task of human beings; as the discovery of humankind's essential divinity it is the deepest meaning of "Christian" reconciliation.

From within these different metanarratives, Kant and Hegel will develop different critiques of religion. For example, Kant will find the creeds of the church deeply problematic, because in telling us what to believe about God they distract us from the only truly religious task, acting rightly toward other human beings. By contrast, Hegel's critique of the creeds will be that they are in the language of the Understanding and are not adequate to the reality they intend, unlike his own System, which speaks the voice of Reason.

Depending on whose philosophy and which religion one finds most persuasive, these metanarratives (and the critiques they imply) will be seen as perfections or parodies of the traditional Christian meganarrative to which they constantly allude.[13] Each is the whole within which the parts of its respective theology take their place. As Schleiermacher reminds us, whole and part stand in a relation of "mutual determination" to each other (see 149). Because this hermeneutical circle can never be closed, because the event of mutual determination can be terminated only arbitrarily, and because the totality whose transparent possession would represent the only nontemporary, nonarbitrary completion of the process always exceeds our grasp, we dwell in one or another of these hermeneutical circles by faith and not by sight. In their own way, Kant and his orthodox Christian predecessors emphasize this fact. In denying it, Hegel looks bold, arrogant, laughable, even desperate, but not convincing. If one wanted to argue that philosophy is the finding of bad reasons for what one believes upon instinct, would there be a better case at hand than Hegel's claim that human thought can be infinite by achieving, not merely anticipating, totality? In the debate between Kant and Hegel and, perhaps, Augustine, we have a conflict of interpretations rather than the conquest of the Idea. Or, to put it a bit differently, we have different faiths seeking understanding.

From the Augustinian tradition we can briefly introduce Kierkegaard into the mix to extend our comparison in a different direction rather than in greater depth. Like Kant's, Kierkegaard's prephilosophical life-world is that of Protestant Pietism. This shows up in the intensely personal and inward relation of the individual to God, in the understanding of sin as willful refusal to live "before God," and in the corresponding rejection of any "pantheistic" definition of sin that takes it to be "something merely negative—weakness, sensuousness, finitude, ignorance, etc." (Kierkegaard, *Sickness* 96).

This last point decisively separates Kierkegaard from Hegel. But he distances himself equally from Kant by finding no need to filter Pietism's understanding of radical human evil through the article of faith most basic to both Kant and Hegel—the autonomy axiom. The faith of his childhood, to which he returned before becoming an author, had *credo ut intelligam* as its motto, not *sapere aude*. Human reason is not self-sufficient—precisely because of sin. Not only because of finitude, but especially because of the noetic effects of sin, human reason not only lacks the power to discover by itself what we need to know for our salvation, but it finds dependence on divine revelation to be offensive, paradoxical, absurd, madness. Faith is not the *pistis* of Plato's divided line or its descendent, the *Vorstellungen* of Hegel's scheme, a deficient mode of knowing that philosophy can make good; it is, rather, the humble courage that is willing to be taught by God what recollection is unable to recollect.[14]

Nor is the human will able to be self-sufficient, except in defiance. Sin is like jumping into a hole too deep to climb out of. Only prevenient grace can effect reconciliation. Thus the paradox that the one who can help "is himself the one who seeks those who have need of help, he is himself the one who goes around and, calling, almost pleading, says: Come here. . . . He does not wait for anyone to come to him; he comes on his own initiative, uncalled" (Kierkegaard, *Practice* 12). In these words we hear Augustine confessing to God, "You converted me to you" (VII:12).

The meganarrative implicit in Kierkegaard's analysis of sin and its forgiveness is a story not of the triumph of the will but of the triumph of that grace which overcomes not only the willfulness that refuses to return to the Good (because it is too busy establishing the Truth), but also the willfulness that insists on converting itself to the Good. Thus there is a critique of the religions of Hegel and Kant. But the most poignant critique of religion that Kierkegaard develops within the framework of this grand narrative is the one known as the attack upon Christendom. It protests, in a Pietistic tone of voice, that life lived before even the most gracious God is far more strenuous than Christendom would like to think and that the complacency that converts grace into "cheap grace" is sin and not faith.

By insisting that this interpretation of our condition is a product of faith that does not even try to establish itself by appeal to some presumptive universal, neutral reason, Kierkegaard suggests that it is presumptuous indeed for Kant to claim that his faith is *grounded* in *pure* practical reason and for Hegel to claim to have gone beyond faith, which everyone has, to knowledge.[15]

***

I have been suggesting that the ways in which philosophy criticizes religion are often the flip side of the ways in which it leads to religion. So I return to Heidegger's previously mentioned claim that theology, as the science of faith, needs philosophy for guidance and *correction*—partly because of its intrinsic interest for our topic and partly because it brings us closer to the question of whether the relation of philosophy to religion is different when that philosophy is phenomenology.

We have seen that for Heidegger, faith is the *Aufhebung* of "pre-faith-full, i.e., unbelieving, human existence" ("Phenomenology" 18). As the science of this recontextualizing reinterpretation, or, if you like, the teleological suspension of unbelieving experience, theology is accordingly *"absolutely different from philosophy"* and, moreover, it is a "fully autonomous ontic science" vis-à-vis philosophy (16; see also 6 and 18). This is what one would expect from a hermeneutical phenomenology according to which the basic beliefs of Christian faith are circularly embedded in a life-world arising from and giving reinforcement to a distinctive combination of practices on the one hand and a meganarrative on the other.

We can only be puzzled when Heidegger exempts phenomenology as ontological science from this *Aufhebung* and leaves it as an independent variable from which Christian theology is to receive both guidance and correction because it is a source of meanings "which can thus be grasped purely rationally" ("Phenomenology" 18). Here we have returned to the Husserlian ideal of philosophy as the rigorous science that can lay the foundation for all of the other sciences. This ideal, as its Cartesian heritage testifies, is a version of the autonomy axiom we encountered in Kant and Hegel and arises within the life-world of the Enlightenment project.[16]

When we turn from this formal claim to the substantive correction that Heidegger offers to theology from this position of authority, we encounter the beginnings of what he will later call the critique of onto-theology. It is a triple critique. First, when philosophical theologies or theological philosophies seek to understand the whole of being with reference to a highest being, they remain in the ontic realm of beings and fall into philosophy's most original sin, *Seinsvergessenheit.* But this is fatal to theology:

> Only from the truth of being can the essence of the holy be thought. Only
> from the essence of the holy is the essence of divinity to be thought. Only in
> the light of the essence of divinity can it be thought or said what the word

"God" is to signify. . . . How can the human being at the present stage of world history ask at all seriously and rigorously whether the god nears or withdraws, when he has above all neglected to think into the dimension in which alone that question can be asked? But this is the dimension of the holy, which indeed remains closed as a dimension if the open region of being is not cleared and in its clearing is near to humans. ("Letter" 267)

The *Seinsmystik* which comes to expression in the claim that the thinking of being must precede the thinking of God, and not vice versa, has its home in the life-world of Romanticism rather than that of Enlightenment. We hear the voice of Hölderlin now, rather than that of Husserl. Much of Romanticism, both English and German, can be seen as a religious quest for a deep source of meaning that exceeds conceptual grasp but is decidedly not the Christian God and, *a fortiori*, is not to be found in the Christian church. But Enlightenment and Romanticism are perhaps best seen not simply as mortal enemies but as the two souls that dwell within the breast of a Faust that we have come to call modernity. Just to the degree that these two souls dwell, as we are now noticing, in Heidegger's breast, we have a thoroughly *modern* Martin.

Jean-Luc Marion is understandably indignant. *Quid juris?* With what right does this hybrid modernity, which comes in postmodern wrapping to be sure, dictate the horizon within which we should think of God? Is not the primacy of being over God a second idolatry, more nearly like than unlike the onto-theologically constituted metaphysics Heidegger critiques (chaps. 2–3)?

Marion's protest is well taken. Heidegger's basic belief in the priority of the being question arises out of two not entirely compatible life-worlds which, in any case, are just that, life-worlds, with all the particularity and contingency that implies, but none of the overarching authority that Heidegger presumes.[17]

But there is another dimension to Heidegger's critique: the second part. In the lecture of 1927–28, we find a sustained critique of theology as a purely theoretical enterprise. "Theology is not speculative knowledge of God" ("Phenomenology" 15). Not only does theology arise out of faithful existence, a life-world of intertwined belief and practice, but it has faithful existence as its goal. "Every theological statement and concept addresses itself *in its very content* to the faith-full existence of the individual in the community; it does *not* do so subsequently, for the sake of some practical '*application*'" ("Phenomenology" 12).

In the later, third part, of the critique, this polemic is further specified. God-talk sells its soul to the devil, thereby becoming onto-theology, when it fails to resist the hegemony of philosophy, according to which "the deity can come into philosophy only insofar as philosophy, of its own accord and by its own nature, requires and determines that and how the deity enters into it" (*Identity* 56). It turns out that philosophy's terms for lending its prestige to God-talk are that God should serve as a means to its end, the project of rendering the whole of being intelligible to human understanding.[18] It is of the god who has been sold into this slavery that Heidegger says, "Man can neither pray nor sacrifice to this god. Before the *causa sui*, man can neither fall to his knees in awe nor can he play music and dance before this god" (*Identity* 72).

This complaint is very different from the *Seinsvergessenheit* critique. We hear the voices of Pascal and Kierkegaard and are reminded of Heidegger's immersion in the New Testament, Luther, and Kierkegaard during the gestation of *Being and Time*. Heidegger has encountered a life-world that is part pre- and part postmodern, but decidedly neither Enlightenment nor Romanticism. And while we cannot say that he really dwells in this life-world of faith, he has become a sufficiently competent player of this language game to be able to speak to us out of it. Now his targets are Aristotle and Hegel, and his critique is the negative moment in the way his philosophy leads to the piety of thinking that is his Romantic religion. Still, if we cannot exactly say that his philosophy leads to the theology of Augustine, or of his Catholic sons Aquinas and Bonaventure, or of his Protestant sons Luther and Calvin (before whose God people do bow in awe, pray and sacrifice, sing and dance), we can say that he opens up a space for their theologies by giving the kind of critique of onto-theology that each of them would welcome, in his own distinctive, nonromantic way.[19]

Biblical, theistic faith has good reason to join Marion in rejecting one dimension of Heidegger's critique, but equally good reason to welcome its other dimension. Any philosophy or theology that would lead to faithful Christian existence needs to affirm divine mystery in the face of onto-theological hubris, a point we can learn not only from Pascal and Kierkegaard, but also from Augustine, from Aquinas and Bonaventure, or from Luther and Calvin.

***

I turn finally to Dominique Janicaud's protest against the "theological turn" in French phenomenology. I have been arguing that philosophy, in spite of its recurrent urge to be pure insight, cannot be presuppositionless, rigorous science. In particular, when it comes to religious matters, it is not pure reason that we encounter in Kant, or Hegel, or Heidegger, but in each case a faith seeking understanding. Is that the case because the first two never knew and the third abandoned the methodical rigor of transcendental phenomenology? Can phenomenology fulfill the dream of being rigorous science if only it remains sufficiently faithful to Husserl? Is the reduction the proper corrective to Descartes's methodical doubt which finally enables us to succeed where he failed? Is eidetic intuition the scene of those clear and distinct ideas which are in fact, as promised, born of immaculate conception?

I think not, and I express my skepticism in a series of questions that will not be surprising in the light of the preceding analysis.

Is not the idea that philosophy can and should be rigorous science itself an article of faith that seeks understanding in transcendental phenomenology? Is it not rooted in an existential desire for security that precedes reflection?[20] Does not this desire arise within an Enlightenment life-world (ancient or modern) that, like the desire to which it gives rise, precedes reflection in its historical particularity and contingency and quickly becomes the tradition that would free thought from tradition? Is not its prejudice against prejudice a dogma (in the nonpejorative sense, a doctrine taught by a church to its initiates) which fails to justify itself by the principle of principles?[21] Is it not, like the verification criterion of meaning in logical positivism, an a priori control belief that cannot satisfy its own requirements?[22]

Another way of asking these questions is to ask whether the history of phenomenology has not been the continual (re)discovery that the ideal of rigorous science is a pipe dream. Does not the almost immediate conversion of transcendental phenomenology into existential and hermeneutical phenomenology show that those who studied Husserl most carefully and took him most seriously were unable to stay with him on this point? Nor is it a matter simply of the rebellion of sons (and grandsons) against the father. Does not Husserl's own development teach us the same lesson? Having discovered the life-world as the horizon of intentional meaning, he tries desperately to neutralize the implications of this discovery by keeping the life-world on the noema side of the equation as a phenomenon to be investigated. But does he not keep discovering, however reluctantly, that the life-world keeps showing up on the noesis side of the equation, insinuating itself into the transcendental ego, giving to it (and thus to philosophical reflection) a historically specific identity, and depriving it of the naked neutrality that Husserl wanted it to retain?[23]

What then, do we find as Janicaud introduces his complaint with a brief history of phenomenology in France? At the beginning of the initial reception, we find the work of Sartre and the early work of Merleau-Ponty. There are two noteworthy features in Janicaud's account. First, he recognizes significant departures from a strict Husserlianism, but these departures do not bother him. On the one hand, he recognizes that there are genuine problems and ambiguities in Husserl's work that generate these departures. In any case, "*Faithful or unfaithful* to the first inspiration, intelligent and provocative works were produced" (21; emphasis added). Second, the atheism of Sartre and Merleau-Ponty does not bother him either, although he explicitly alludes to it. He praises "the limits of the first French phenomenological 'breakthrough'" (17) without any tirade against, say, *Being and Nothingness* as a "rupture with immanent phenomenality" (17). The same tone continues in the brief discussion of the later work of Merleau-Ponty.

But all hell breaks loose when we come to a work contemporary with *The Visible and the Invisible*: Levinas's *Totality and Infinity*. As Bernard Prusak puts it in his introduction to the English translation of *The Theological Turn*, Janicaud puts Levinas on trial, charged with corrupting youth—namely, the "new phenomenologists," Marion, Chrétien, and Henry (3). Janicaud acknowledges that Levinas is "responding to the same deficiency of Husserlian phenomenology" (25) as is Merleau-Ponty and that in both cases the tactics "consist . . . in being more faithful to the spirit of phenomenology than Husserl himself" (26). Yet it is only to Levinas that Janicaud attributes "an attitude which loftily affirms itself" (25).

The rhetorical barrage intensifies as the contrast is drawn:

> Between the unconditional affirmation of Transcendence and the patient interrogation of the visible, the incompatibility cries out; we must choose. But are we going to do so with the head or the heart—arbitrarily or not? The task, in so far as it remains philosophical and phenomenological, is to follow the sole guide that does not buy itself off with fine words. . . . [Merleau-Ponty's] way presupposes nothing other than an untiring desire for elucidation of that which most hides itself away in experience. . . .
>
> On the contrary, the directly dispossessing aplomb of alterity supposes a non-phenomenological, metaphysical desire; it comes from "a land not of our birth."[24] It supposes a metaphysico-theological montage, prior to philosophical writing. The dice are loaded and choices made; faith rises majestically in the background. The reader, confronted by the blade of the absolute, finds him or herself in a position of a catechumen who has no other choice than to penetrate the holy words and lofty dogmas. (26–27)

We are reminded of Philip Rieff's commentary on Freud:

> It is on the subject of religion that the judicious clinician grows vehement and disputatious. Against no other stronghold of repressive culture are the reductive weapons of psychoanalysis deployed in such open hostility. Freud's customary detachment fails him here. Confronting religion, psychoanalysis shows itself for what it is: the last great formulation of nineteenth-century secularism, complete with substitute doctrine and cult. (281)

If we ask what has triggered the replacement of detachment with such vehemence and open hostility in Janicaud's narrative, the answer is not far to seek. Levinas tells us that metaphysical desire is "for the absolutely other [*Autre*]" understood as "the alterity of the Other [*Autrui*] and of the Most-High" (34). What is here "imposed from the outset," Janicaud tells us, is "nothing less than the God of the biblical tradition" (27).

This is a highly dubious claim. Whether one is thinking of the Jewish or the Christian Bible, one cannot, without a lot of wishful thinking, find the God of the Bible in a text that tells us, "It is our relations with men . . . that give to theological concepts the sole signification they admit of. . . . Everything that cannot be reduced to an interhuman relation represents not the superior form but the forever primitive form of religion" (79). Both Jewish and Christian scriptures make it clear that we cannot truly love God unless we *also* love our neighbor, but neither reduces the former to the latter.

But this is beside the point. Whether rightly or wrongly, Janicaud is convinced that Levinas has introduced the biblical God into philosophical discourse, and this is the cause of his apoplectic accusation: "Strict treason of the reduction that handed over the transcendental I to its nudity" (27). The earlier questions recur. Does not the desire for philosophy to be carried out by the transcendental I in its nudity itself arise prior to philosophical writing? In the project of transcendental phenomenology are not the dice loaded and choices made in favor of reason's autonomy? Does not a certain "faith rise majestically in the background" so that we find ourselves addressed as catechumens (or perhaps heretics)?

A second kind of question arises. When Levinas's (alleged) theism is denounced as treason against the reduction rather than as "patient interrogation of the visible" and as "an untiring desire for elucidation of that which most hides itself away in experience" (27), why is the atheism of Sartre and Merleau-Ponty, which is far less ambiguous than Levinas's theism, given a free pass? When we are told that religious belief compromises rational objectivity but that religious unbelief does not, is this the voice of pure reason or the voice of the life-world of Enlightenment secularism into which a particular speaker has been socialized?

The story is told of a boy who told his father of the narrow escape his dog had when chased by a very angry and much larger dog. The smaller dog just climbed up a tree to safety. In response to the father's protest that dogs cannot climb trees, the boy responded, "But Daddy, he just got to." It has always seemed to me that there is a lot of "But Daddy, he just got to" in the Husserlian project of philosophy as rigorous science. What persuades is not the clear vision of the dog in the tree, the intuition of the actualization of the ideal, but a desperate vision of the psychologism and historicism that will befall us if the dog cannot climb the tree. So, in response to the evidence (a good Husserlian term) that the transcendental ego is not naked after all but thoroughly wrapped in psychological and historical contingencies of life-world and meganarrative proportions, the true-believer [sic] replies, "But it just got to be naked!"

One cannot simply ignore this vertigo of relativity that has terrorized philosophers at least since Plato. Is the only alternative to complete transcendence of the cave sophistry, cynicism, even nihilism? I think not, and conclude with the briefest sketch of what I think philosophy can be if it cannot be the nude dancing of egos so transcendental that they raise new questions about the identity of indiscernibles.

Philosophy will be perspectival rather than pure. As interpretation rather than intuition, it will continue to be what it has always been, the conflict of interpretations. But this need not reduce us to the method of tenacity. If thought has the finitude implied in the impossibility of being pure reason, then each of us has good reason to think that we might learn something from the other, and this is the best rationale for conversation that is not chatter but a serious meeting of the minds.

Conversational reason is dialogical rather than monological; correspondingly, the emphasis shifts from taking a concrete individual and making it [sic] abstract (nude) to the ethics of intersubjective relations. The ethics of such conversation is no doubt a virtue ethics. Habermas reminds us of the virtue of fairness.[25] Gadamer reminds us of the virtue of open-mindedness.[26] Linda Zagzebski gives major attention to both of these virtues (among many others) in her virtue epistemology. When our interpretations are in conflict, the possibility of my learning from you presupposes that I enter the conversation with a considerable degree of these two virtues.

But in this conversation I am both teacher and learner, and I am responsible for presenting my own interpretations as faithfully as possible to the other, whom I must presuppose to be both fair and open-minded. This involves articulation and testimony. By articulation, I mean what I hinted at in the earlier reference to vision and articulation—namely, spelling out the whole of which this or that belief is a part as fully as possible, giving the big picture in pictures, where appropriate, as well as in arguments that display the inner logic of my position. Thus, for example, while Kierkegaard's Climacus sees Christian faith as opposed to worldly understanding, his Anti-Climacus speaks of "faith's understanding" (*Practice* 78), and Kierkegaard's entire corpus, pseudonymous and not, is best read as a setting forth of the inner rationale of Christian faith and practice (which, to repeat, knows itself to be faith and not pure reason). The intellectual virtues at issue here are clarity and honesty: clarity in making my perspective as transparent as possible and honesty in not compromising that transparency by hiding anything.

By testimony, I mean presenting my perspective as a first-person report, saying, "This is how it looks from where I stand, which, of course, does not afford the view from nowhere; if you look carefully, can't you see pretty much the same thing?" I do not purport to be the judge or jury, much less the Supreme Court. I am simply one who has taken the stand to tell what I have seen and to answer questions, both friendly and hostile, as best I can. The intellectual virtue at issue here is obviously humility.

This is, as promised, only a sketch. These themes need much fuller exploration, and, important as I believe them to be, I do not for a moment think that they exhaust the nature of conversational reason. My own view is that the project of spelling out the middle ground between absolute knowledge and cynical nihilism is and has been a major preoccupation of twentieth-century philosophy across a variety of traditions and vocabularies. That task is anything but completed. My persuasion is that we are best equipped to understand and contribute to that conversation about conversation when we realize the degree to which reason is always already faith.

NOTES

1. The complexity, and even incoherence, of these beliefs stems from the fact that beginning with our most immediate family, we are socialized into a variety of communities that are not necessarily compatible; we gain competence in many language games.

2. For the views sketched below, Plantinga, "Reason"; *Current Debate*, especially chapter 4; and *Proper Function*, especially chapter 10.

3. Peirce introduces this notion in "Fixation" (235). To avoid having his theory identified as fideism in some such sense, Plantinga prefers to say that when basic beliefs are true and the product of a properly functioning cognitive apparatus of the right sort and in the right circumstances, they are products of reason.

4. At A 738 = B 766 we read, "Reason must in all its undertakings subject itself to criticism; should it limit freedom of criticism by any prohibitions, it must harm itself, drawing upon itself a damaging suspicion. Nothing is so important through its usefulness, nothing so sacred, that it may be exempted from this searching examination, which knows no respect for persons." In a surprisingly Habermasian tone of voice, Kant continues, "For reason has no dictatorial authority; its verdict is always simply the agreement of free citizens, of whom each one must be permitted to express, without let or hindrance, his objections or even his veto."

5. In keeping what has here been called the Wittgensteinian/Foucauldian theme, Heidegger notes that the *positum* of Christian theology, as a positive science, "is come upon in a definite prescientific manner of approaching and proceeding with that which is," that "this disclosure is prior to any theoretical consideration," and that it is "already illuminated and guided by an understanding of Being—even if it be nonconceptual" ("Phenomenology" 7).

6. Heidegger even adds that faith "is in its innermost core the mortal enemy of the *form of existence* which is an essential part of *philosophy*. . . . Faith is so absolutely the mortal enemy that philosophy does not even begin to want in any way to do battle with it. This factual *existentiell opposition* between faithfulness and a human's free appropriation of his whole existence . . ." ("Phenomenology" 20).

7. Helpful discussion of this motif is found in Van Buren, *Young Heidegger*, and Kisiel. See also Van Buren, "Ethics."

8. In the chapter of that title in *Why I Am Not a Christian*.

9. We have already seen Heidegger, following Kierkegaard's Climacus—and, for that matter, Augustine and Paul—link faith in this sense to rebirth. This distinguishes it from the *pistis* of Plato's divided line (and much Enlightenment thinking) which is merely a defective form of knowing. For this tradition, treating faith as a defective form of knowing has its analog in Aristotle's treating woman as a defective form of man; it signifies a violent hegemony.

10. Both Kant and Hegel find it necessary to relate their theologies to biblical narratives, contrasting their hermeneutics of reason with unenlightened interpretations.

11. Cf. 307 and Addition 3 to ¶24 of the Encyclopedia *Logic*. I have discussed this matter in greater detail in "Hegel."

12. I have discussed the crucial correspondence of 1795 in "*Von Hegel bis Hegel*." On 26 January 1795, Hölderlin wrote to Hegel, "[Fichte's] Absolute Self, which equals Spinoza's Substance, contains all reality; it is everything, and outside it, is nothing. There is thus no object for this Absolute Self, since otherwise all reality would not be in it. Yet a consciousness without an object is inconceivable. . . . Thus, in the Absolute Self no consciousness is conceivable" (*Hegel: The Letters* 33).

13. The traditional Christian story is a grand narrative indeed, but it is not a metanarrative in Lyotard's sense for at least the following reasons. 1) It is not a meta-discourse but a first-order discourse, kerygma not apologetics. 2) Its proper function is not to legitimize modernity's practices of knowledge and politics but to delegitimize all human practices not completely in harmony with the Kingdom of God (which is not a

human production). Accordingly, 3) it is told by prophets and apostles, who make no pretense to being the voice of human reason, rather than by philosophers, who do.

14. It is of interest in this connection that in the concluding paragraph of the *Phenomenology of Spirit*, Hegel describes Absolute Knowing in terms of recollection. Cf. the passage in which Augustine describes what he did *not* find in the books of the Platonists, which leads him to describe Platonic wisdom as "presumption" rather than "confession" (*Confessions* VII:9 and 20).

15. Hegel tells his students, "Religion is for everyone. It is not philosophy, which is not for everyone" (1:180). Cf. the polemic against going "beyond faith" in the preface and epilogue to Kierkegaard's *Fear and Trembling*.

16. The surprisingly Cartesian character of Heidegger's thought shows up in another way in his analysis of guilt and the call of conscience in *Being and Time*, ¶¶54–60. The ontological analysis, according to which the call of conscience is the call of *Dasein* to itself, is both prior to and the condition for the possibility of ontic understandings of conscience as the voice of God, or of parents, or of society at large. But this means that *Dasein's* relation to itself is prior to and the condition of its relation to the Other, human or divine, a Cartesian thesis that would be hotly contested by such diverse thinkers as Hegel, Kierkegaard, Levinas, and Sartre, for whom there is no immediate self-presence and for whom the Other always stands between me and myself. The inner sanctum of the prereflective cogito has always already been invaded by the Other.

17. In due course, when the critique of onto-theology comes to be named as such, Heidegger will also articulate the *Seinsgeschichte*, the metanarrative to which his basic belief belongs.

18. The analysis of representational and calculative thinking in such texts as *The Principle of Reason* and *Discourse on Thinking*, and *The Question Concerning Technology* is a sustained critique of this project.

19. If Aquinas's God, for example, were nothing but an Unmoved Mover, he might well be convicted of onto-theology. But in a Hegelian fashion, as we move through the *Summa*, that abstract initial description is continually concretized, personalized, and rendered fit for genuinely religious worship. And the last thing that any of these theologies do is use God to make the whole of being fully intelligible to human understanding. I have discussed the issues raised by Heidegger's critique in greater detail in "Overcoming Ontotheology."

20. Thus Adorno suggests that "the totally unobvious need for absolute spiritual security . . . [is] the reflex to real powerlessness and insecurity" (15). Cf. Derrida's claim that the lack of foundation "is basic and nonempirical and that the security of presence in the metaphorical form of ideality arises and is set forth again upon this irreducible void" (7).

21. The "prejudice against prejudice" (against prejudgment or, perhaps, faith as I've used the term) formula comes, of course, from Gadamer (see 270). Husserl's Principle of All Principles is given in ¶24 of *Ideas* (44).

22. Thus Feigl explains that the empiricist criterion of meaning "does not fall under its own jurisdiction" because it is to be understood "as a proposal and not as a proposition" (15). For the long narrative which leads, ever so reluctantly, to this conclusion, see Hempel.

23. For this narrative, see Landgrebe. This essay should be read with the Hempel essay cited in the previous note.

24. This is a citation from Levinas 33–34.

25. Like most analytic epistemologists he speaks in a deontological tone of voice. I am suggesting that his norms can be read as descriptions of a virtue.

26. Risser highlights this dimension in *Hermeneutics.*

WORKS CITED

Adorno, Theodor W. *Against Epistemology: A Metacritique: Studies in Husserl and the Phenomenological Antinomies.* Trans. Willis Domingo. Cambridge: MIT Press, 1982.

Augustine. *Confessions.* Trans. Rex Warner. New York: New American Library, 1963.

Derrida, Jacques. *Speech and Phenomena and Other Essays on Husserl's Theory of Signs.* Trans. David B. Allison. Evanston: Northwestern University Press, 1973.

Feigl, Herbert. "Some Major Issues and Developments in the Philosophy of Science of Logical Empiricism." In Herbert Feigl and Michael Scriven, eds., *The Foundations of Science and the Concepts of Psychology and Psychoanalysis,* 3–37. Minnesota Studies in the Philosophy of Science, Vol. 1. Minneapolis: University of Minnesota Press, 1956.

Gadamer, Hans-Georg. *Truth and Method.* 2nd rev. ed. Trans. Joel Weinsheimer and Donald G. Marshall. New York: Crossroad, 1991.

Hegel, Georg Wilhelm Friedrich. *Lectures on the Philosophy of Religion.* Vols. 1 and 3. Trans. and ed. Peter. C. Hodgson. Berkeley: University of California Press, 1984–87.

——. *Enzyklopädie der philosophischen Wissenschaften, Erster Teil, Die Wissenschaft der Logik mit den mündlichen Zusätzen.* Vol. 8 of *G. W. F. Hegel Werke in zwanzig Bänden.* Ed. Eva Moldenhauer and Karl Markus Michel. Frankfurt a.M.: Suhrkamp, 1970.

Heidegger, Martin. *Being and Time.* Trans. John Macquarrie and Edward Robinson. New York: Harper & Row, 1962.

——. *Discourse on Thinking.* Trans. John M. Anderson and E. Hans Freund. New York: Harper & Row, 1966.

——. *Identity and Difference.* Trans. Joan Stambaugh. New York: Harper & Row, 1969.

——. "Letter on 'Humanism.'" In *Pathmarks,* ed. William McNeill, 239–276. Cambridge: Cambridge University Press, 1998.

——. "Phenomenology and Theology." In *The Piety of Thinking,* trans. James G. Hart and John C. Maraldo, 5–21. Bloomington: Indiana University Press, 1976.

——. *The Principle of Reason.* Trans. Reginald Lilly. Bloomington: Indiana University Press, 1991.

——. *The Question Concerning Technology and Other Essays.* Trans. William Lovitt. New York: Harper & Row, 1977.

Hempel, C. G. "Problems and Changes in the Empiricist Criterion of Meaning." In Leonard Linsky, ed., *Semantics and the Philosophy of Language: A Collection of Readings.* Urbana: University of Illinois Press, 1952.

Hölderlin, Friedrich. "Letter, 26 January 1795." In G. W. F. Hegel, *Hegel: The Letters,* trans. Clark Butler and Christine Seiler, 33–34. Bloomington: Indiana University Press, 1984.

Husserl, Edmund. *Ideas Pertaining to a Pure Phenomenology and a Phenomenological Philosophy, First Book*. Trans. F. Kersten. Boston: Martinus Nijhoff, 1982.

Janicaud, Dominique. *The Theological Turn in French Phenomenology*. Trans. Bernard G. Prusack. In Dominique Janicaud, Jean-François Courtine, Jean-Louis Chrétien, Michel Henry, Jean-Luc Marion, and Paul Ricoeur, *Phenomenology and the "Theological Turn": The French Debate*, 16–103. New York: Fordham University Press, 2000.

Kant, Immanuel. *The Critique of Pure Reason*. Trans. Norman Kemp Smith. New York: Macmillan, 1961.

———. *Grounding for the Metaphysics of Morals*. 2nd ed. Trans. James W. Ellington. Indianapolis: Hackett, 1981.

———. *Religion Within the Limits of Reason Alone*. 2nd ed. Trans. Theodore M. Greene and Hoyt H. Hudson. New York: Harper & Brothers, 1960.

Kierkegaard, Søren. *Concluding Unscientific Postscript*. Trans. Howard V. Hong and Edna H. Hong. Princeton: Princeton University Press, 1992.

———. *Practice in Christianity*. Trans. Howard V. Hong and Edna H. Hong. Princeton: Princeton University Press, 1991.

———. *The Sickness unto Death: A Christian Psychological Exposition for Upbuilding and Awakening*. Trans. Howard V. Hong and Edna H. Hong. Princeton: Princeton University Press, 1980.

Kisiel, Theodore. *The Genesis of Heidegger's* Being and Time. Berkeley: University of California Press, 1993.

Landgrebe, Ludwig. "Husserl's Departure from Cartesianism." Trans. R. V. Elveton. In Donn Welton, ed., *The Phenomenology of Edmund Husserl: Six Essays*, 66–121. Ithaca, N.Y.: Cornell University Press, 1981.

Levinas, Emmanuel. *Totality and Infinity: An Essay on Exteriority*. Trans. Alphonso Lingis. Pittsburgh: Duquesne University Press, 1969.

Lyotard, Jean-François. *The Postmodern Condition: A Report on Knowledge*. Trans. Geoff Bennington and Brian Massumi. Minneapolis: Minnesota University Press, 1984.

Marion, Jean-Luc. *God Without Being*. Trans. Thomas A. Carlson. Chicago: University of Chicago Press, 1991.

Marx, Karl. Introduction to "Towards a Critique of Hegel's *Philosophy of Right*." In *Karl Marx: Selected Writings*, ed. David McLellan, 63–74. New York: Oxford University Press, 1977.

Peirce, Charles Sanders. "The Fixation of Belief." In *Collected Papers of Charles Sanders Peirce*, Vol. 5, ed. Charles Hartshorne and Paul Weiss, 223–247. Cambridge: Harvard University Press, 1960.

Plantinga, Alvin. "Reason and Belief in God." In *The Analytic Theist: An Alvin Plantinga Reader*, ed. James F. Sennett, 102–161. Grand Rapids: Eerdmans, 1998.

———. *Warrant: The Current Debate*. New York: Oxford University Press, 1993.

———. *Warrant and Proper Function*. New York: Oxford University Press, 1993.

Prusak, Bernard G. Translator's introduction to *The Theological Turn of French Phenomenology*, by Dominique Janicaud. In Dominique Janicaud, Jean-François Courtine, Jean-Louis Chrétien, Michel Henry, Jean-Luc Marion, and Paul Ricoeur, *Phenomenology and the "Theological Turn": The French Debate*, 3–15. New York: Fordham University Press, 2000.

Rieff, Philip. *Freud: The Mind of the Moralist.* Garden City, N.Y.: Doubleday, 1961.

Risser, James. *Hermeneutics and the Voice of the Other: Re-reading Gadamer's Philosophical Hermeneutics.* Albany: SUNY Press, 1997.

Russell, Bertrand. "A Free Man's Worship." In idem, *Why I Am Not a Christian,* 3–23. New York: Simon and Schuster, 1957.

Ryle, Gilbert. *The Concept of Mind.* New York: Barnes & Noble, 1949.

Schleiermacher, Friedrich. *Hermeneutics and Criticism and Other Writings.* Trans. and ed. Andrew Bowie. Cambridge: Cambridge University Press, 1998.

Van Buren. John. "The Ethics of *Formale Anzeige* in *Being and Time.*" *American Catholic Philosophical Quarterly* 69, No. 2 (Spring 1995): 157–170.

———. *The Young Heidegger: Rumor of the Hidden King.* Bloomington: Indiana University Press, 1994.

Westphal, Merold. "Hegel: The Hermeneutics of 'Christian' Pantheism." In the *Blackwell Companion to Theology.* Oxford: Blackwell, forthcoming.

———. "Overcoming Ontotheology." In *Overcoming Onto-Theology: Toward a Postmodern Christian Faith,* 1–28. New York: Fordham University Press, 2001.

———. "*Von Hegel bis Hegel:* Reflections on 'The Earliest System-Programme of German Idealism.'" In Michael Baur and Daniel O. Dahlstrom, eds., *The Emergence of German Idealism,* 269–287. Washington, D.C.: Catholic University of America, 1999.

Wolterstorff, Nicholas. *Reason within the Bounds of Religion.* Grand Rapids: Eerdmans, 1976.

Zagzebski, Linda Trinkaus. *Virtues of the Mind: An Inquiry into the Nature of Virtue and the Ethical Foundations of Knowledge.* Cambridge: Cambridge University Press, 1996.

The Question into Meaning and the Question of God

A Hermeneutic Approach

Ben Vedder

In philosophy today there is a great deal of discussion about man's knowledge of God. Generally, one can say that the classical discrepancy between faith and reason is always present in the background of that discussion. The God of the Bible is placed in a position diametrically opposed to the God of the philosophers, mirroring the relation between religion and philosophy. However, according to Jean-Luc Marion, this relation is an impossible one: "The field of religion could simply be defined as what philosophy excludes or, in the best case, subjugates" ("Phénomène" 79 [103[1]]). In this view, the task of the philosophy of religion is to objectify, and with that it loses its object as a religious object: "Either it would be a question of phenomena that are objectively definable but lose their religious specificity, or it would be a question of phenomena that are specifically religious but cannot be described objectively" (ibid.). A philosophical understanding of religious words such as the word *God* implies that they are no longer religious words, but neutralized philosophical concepts.

I will discuss this dichotomy in terms of the relationship between meaning and being: Is it possible to come to God by means of a philosophical approach to being? Does every ontology end in natural theology? The usual presupposition is that God can be found by thinking about being; every ontology would end in a theology. Or is it that the meaning supplied by revelation and tradition has no need for the question of being?[2]

It is impossible to imagine contemporary culture without God, whoever or whatever is understood by that term. The word, or concept *God* is present in and linked with various convictions, representations, ideas, and philosophical concepts. Thus, within the context of this culture, the question of the being and meaning of God arises. However, it usually arises as a question of whether God's existence can be proven conclusively—whether it is possible, with rational means, to allot to God a reality that will also convince others. Or is it that, here in particular, faith and conviction on the one hand, and *ratio* on the other, have little impact on one another? In the domain of faith, is it not, rather, that no one will be convinced by rational evidence? In what follows, I will develop the importance of the rational question as a question into the reality of the meaning that forms the basis on which people lead meaningful lives. I will then apply these observations to the philosophical question of God. Finally, I will ask whether the philosophical question of God will lose its original, meaningful context unless it is linked up again to its point of departure.

Meaning and Being

Under the influence of phenomenology and hermeneutics, we understand that there is no observation or reality to which no previous meaning has been attached. The bare question into being does not exist because being is always given within a context of meaning. Therefore, the reason for the question into being always has its basis in a concrete context of meaning. It follows that it is a misconception to assume that a reflective speaking which seeks to be meaningful starts with meaningless being.

All talk about reality is embedded in a previous framework of meaning that motivates and enables this speaking. Proofs always come too late here. The question about the basis of being is possible only within the question of meaning. The meaning that can be perceived by a human being must already have been attuned to that human being. It is obvious that meaning cannot be found in the formal determination of the always receding perspective of thinking, wanting, and feeling. After all, thinking is always motivated by the particular contents that fascinate it. Thinking always stands in a tradition that provides it with themes and points of orientation. In one way or another, human beings are always attuned to the meaning that emerges in their lives. How else would they be able to recognize it?

First comes the meaning that motivates human beings, based on which they question its truth and reality. In a certain sense, this means we follow that meaning and respond to it. I cannot overtake what motivates me, for what attracts me eludes me. Every definitive interpretation of it is premature. We come too late because it has already gone before; we are too early because we act prematurely in relation to that which cannot be caught up with: meaning as a receding perspective.

Such a description of the relation between meaning and being is the result of an experience *with* meaning, an experience that shows that the human being is not self-oriented but oriented toward the other. In that sense, we are oriented toward what has preceded us. This experience with meaning gives insight into the structure of meaning within the framework in which we are offered meaning. This formal structure is not itself the content of the meaning or the substantive meaningful motive.[3] The experience *with* meaning shows that a human being can be oriented toward what has gone before. In the experience of searching for meaning, thinking is continually drawn beyond its own boundaries; it is an experience of transcendence. The experience of transcendence, however, is not itself the substantive motive that provides meaning. This transcendence can be experienced on the basis of various motives of meaning. However, when aiming for the experience of transcendence as such, we risk losing these original motivations of meaning. That is the fate that can strike the outsider, the spectator, the philosopher, who is not personally involved in the meaning. In this way, the philosopher describes and illustrates the condition of possibility for a meaning that precedes the human being, but he or she does this formally, without getting involved in the substantive meaning. Here I differentiate between "transcendentology," as the realm of the philosopher, and the motives of meaning out of which people live. The philosopher has his or her own domain.

Indeed, to be a philosopher is to distance oneself from any motivating fascination in order to gain insight into the formal structure of meaning. The philosopher's motivation lies in thinking, not in a differentiated meaning. Thinking and determining transcendence is the specific task of philosophy. That the God of the philosophers sometimes is made accessible and understandable with certain notions of transcendence does not follow from the nature of the Godhead but from the specific philosophical approach that makes it accessible. The philosopher determines, first, the formal structure of meaning, as we observe in Heidegger's analysis of *Dasein*. From him we learn that "Being is *transcendens* pure and simple" (Heidegger 38 [62]).

There is a lesson to be learned from the experience with meaning and with transcendence. Indeed, against the background of the experience with transcendence and in the question into the substantive interpretation of transcendence—in other words, in the concrete fascination with the substantive meaning that attracts and motivates me—we know that any definitive meaning is a product of myopia. We learn that every interpretation is temporary. Those who appeal to a definitive meaning will eventually fail because they cut themselves off from the different, the unfamiliar, the unexpected that may yet emerge from the riches that meaning has in store. The same goes for the believer and for the thinker who is searching for the meaning of the word *God*,

37

a word that has been handed down in stories that give believers and philosophers food for thought. In philosophy as transcendentology, we learn that we should not be too quick to identify the ultimate meaning of meaningful words.

In our culture, the person who wants to think about God will always do so through previous stories that have evolved through the effect and development of earlier statements. The God who has been handed down in these narratives is not exclusively the God of the philosophers, whose being is argued philosophically. Any talk about God that is exclusively philosophical is cut off from talk about God as present in our culture as a motive of thinking. Talk about God that is exclusively philosophical ignores the preceding meaning-inspiring origin that motivates its thinking. It tends to identify theology with what I call transcendentology, as in the onto-theological tradition. It is true that the onto-theological tradition discusses the being of God, but its motive for doing so is not included in its reflection. In contrast, within a hermeneutic context, the question of God's existence originates neither in the question of being nor in the question of transcendence, but in the question of God as he has been made known traditionally in narratives. The question of God's existence aims at gaining insight into the reality of that which is questioned. For a human being looking for insight, the meaningfulness and validity of one's insight increases with one's knowledge concerning the being of God and with one's discovery that the object of one's thinking is not an illusion. What is important is that the question of being is motivated by the question of the validity and relevance of meaning. From the perspective of meaning, the question of being has an apologetic character. One asks the question to strengthen the position of the meaning.

A Motivated Question of Being

Without wishing to assert that proofs of God can bring about a religious conversion in a person, it is nonetheless important to define the relation between philosophical reflection on being and reflection on the human attribution of meaning. Probably no one has ever been converted as a result of a theoretical proof of God's existence. As, first, philosophy or ontology, philosophy aims not at making converts but at knowledge of existence, of being qua being, and of transcendence. But what meaning does the question of being have in relation to the experience and offer of meaning?

Is it necessary, as is sometimes suggested, to dismiss every relation between insight and meaning as irrelevant (as in Burms and De Dijn)? I think it is not. (And in this I agree with Steel.) We can say that the meaning of the Santa Claus ritual for children has everything to do with a particular theoretical conviction concerning the reality, the existence, and the actions of this saint. When a child reaches an age of discernment, there will be a crisis in the experience of meaning. This phenomenon shows that there is a relation between insight—in other words, knowledge concerning the reality of a being—and the experience of meaning. This is even more prominent in the world of grown-ups and in what is referred to as an adult religion. A relationship between people based on the meaning of love and mutual recognition is undermined when the theoretical insight of one partner moves toward becoming an insight that the love and recognition of the other partner are just a delusion. It is difficult to determine how this relation between theoretical insight and meaning is definitive, but it seems obvious that there is a relation for the person who thinks and seeks meaning. After all, if the loss or change of a theoretical insight has an impact on the experience of meaning as indicated above, we may safely conclude that the experience of meaning is clearly associated with particular insights. Theoretical insights into reality and human-being codetermine—in fact, can radically change—what a person considers to be meaningful. This means also that theoretical insight into transcendence has consequences for the way that I understand the meaning that motivates my questions. However, theoretical insight and meaning are not the same.

It seems that the philosophical approach to God loses its relation to the original meaning by thinking about God's being and transcendence; it becomes transcendentology. A closer look into the motivating context of this philosophical doctrine of God is, therefore, important. There may be reasons for preferring theoretical and philosophical insight over the coincidence and capriciousness of historical reality. Similarly, natural theology stands in a context that has its own meaningful motives. Natural theology is not any more separately available than is any other theology. It also has a context from which it is motivated. In the seventeenth century, natural theology tried to distinguish itself from positive historical theology, in particular, by claiming to found itself on the human being's ability to think. Indeed, it seemed that natural theology would lose its context—namely, faith; it rejected tradition and wanted explicitly to distinguish itself from revealed faith. Natural theology took up a position against the concrete historical religion of European Christianity. The motivating context of the philosophy of God was no longer sought in, and on the basis of, religion, but in rational thinking.

Spinoza was the champion of natural theology. His main theological concern was to find a position from where he could transcend the differences between religions and moral traditions, matters strongly differentiated in place and time. The folly of religious intolerance led to the realization, "Never again!" Spinoza sought an ideal in which religious intolerance would end and human society would realize the ideal of peace. In his opinion, positive historical religion guaranteed disagreement, prejudice, and discrimination among people. However, he believed that human beings could realize a time of peace if positive religion would listen to natural reason. We can understand the meaning-framework and the motive that form the basis of this theoretical approach to natural theology to be the emancipation of thinking. The awareness of freedom was the most important thing (cf. Peperzak). Hearsay (which, according to Spinoza, includes reading the Bible) and information based on superficial observation make human beings slaves of prejudice. Emancipation from that slavery comes only through knowing that which governs the whole of reality, through knowing timeless laws. Unlike hearsay and knowledge from authority, the knowledge of nature can be attained by anyone; it is not esoteric or elitist. Thus, according to Spinoza, through the knowledge of nature, it is possible to emancipate the human being as a thinking individual from the narrow-mindedness of prejudice and misunderstanding. The theoretical insights built up by human beings concerning the reality and the entirety of being liberate them from slavish and blind faith in authoritarian powers and institutions.

Such thinking deserves respect. The context and meaning of seventeenth-century natural theology should be judged on the basis of its own specific approach. It takes its motive from the search for a rationality and reality that are accessible to all; in its case, in other words, a meaningful motive for the philosophy of God is found in thinking. However, it is clear that the meaning of the faith that motivates theology has significantly changed from what it was, for example, with Anselm. What remains is the fact of being or the motivating context from which the philosophical question of God emerges without going beyond the boundaries of this motivating context itself.

The relation between meaning and theoretical insight is clearest when we listen to the thinkers commonly referred to as the masters of suspicion: Marx, Nietzsche, and Freud. Their theoretical insights with respect to religion and meaning have led to a crisis in meaning and religious experience, precisely where natural theology thought to introduce a universally valid reality. They showed that the knowledge of reality and of human being, given to us as something universally valid, was in fact a formulation of a concrete, historical, and individual interest. They also corrected and criticized religious thinking that claimed that religion is the highest meaning. As a result, they went beyond the emancipatory tendency that was already present in natural theology. Thinking that searches for the foundations of the issue that it studies tries to free religious thinking from ambiguities, and *in this it is motivated by the very issue that is studied.* The issue that the thinking person focuses on is that which stimulates thinking without being engulfed by the thinking process. The road taken by thinking is, therefore, a road of loss and recuperation. Against this background, it appears that theoretical reason has not definitively come to terms with the meaning of reality. In thinking, human beings search for new insights about the meaning of reality, and in this search it becomes clear that theoretical reasoning does not stop in a particular place. This means that thinking human beings learn to let go of or even lose some things that they have discovered, because they are looking for a better insight into that which motivates them and which they take to be meaningful. This search does not end when its object has been discovered.

The attempt, in thinking, to say something about God is motivated by the issue that fascinates thinking and that therefore must also be criticized, supplemented, or corrected by this thinking. This does not mean that God belongs to the exclusive domain, inaccessible to thinking, of theology or faith. Philosophers who want to say something about God will approach their theme through *thinking*—in other words, in searching for grounds, foundations, or phenomenological descriptions. Especially as thinkers confronted with the limits of their thinking, philosophers can come to the conclusion that God manifests himself as an unfathomable foundation. To use another metaphor, philosophers can reach this conclusion when they search for light, as an unapproachable light. Only the one who searches for grounds can perceive something as unfathomable. As for many who came after him, it was Plato's experience—and we certainly cannot say that he was not a thinker—that thinking must not culminate in grasping and controlling. Thinking learns that what it wins will be lost again. Thinking can also be an expectant and hopeful opening up to the things that one cannot appropriate at will but which must be offered to and conferred on a person as an insight and an apt formulation because thinking eludes self-willed thinking. Plato's understanding of *eros* is a thinking that gives one the full expectation of receiving that which may suddenly appear. With Plato, great thinkers have always pointed out that the ultimate is received as truth and that it is not within the scope of human anticipation and control. The same thought is reflected in the way that Anselm describes what gave him the thought of the ontological proof of God's existence. In his preface to the *Proslogion* (33), he describes how he had already given up his search when the thought which he had been looking for began to urge itself upon him irresistibly.

Thinking does not begin without antecedents; it is always motivated by an issue that presents itself. This is equally true for thinking about God. In Western culture and religion, God was communicated to human beings in historical statements echoed in the stories handed down in a particular tradition. This message and these stories are the point of departure for the question into the meaning of human existence. In these stories, we also touch upon that which, or the person who, is referred to with the word *God*. The meaning that is taken as a point of departure appears to be a prior point of orientation that cannot be determined definitively. That is why it continues to give rise to new meanings and new questions. The question into being and reality is also motivated by a prior meaning-establishing narrative that has already been spoken.

I understand Anselm to be saying the same thing. Thus, I can formulate my position regarding Anselm by quoting from Martin Moors:

> Every interpretation that ignores the hermeneutic-regulative meaning of the introductory invocative prayer in the *Proslogion* can only spell out the meanings of the adduced arguments (*id quo maius cogitare non possit*).

> However, the philosophical lucidity that this spelling exercise is supposed to yield fulfils no purpose whatsoever. Therefore, it does not in any way serve the purpose of that sacred truth that Anselm, in thinking, labored so hard to understand. (209; my translation)

The question of whether God is the highest being always occurs within the scope of meaning in which this question arises. Anselm already knew God from the faith that had been preached to him. It is therefore strange that, as theology asks about the being of God, the question is continually abstracted away from the context of faith. In rational theology, God, as proclaimed in the traditional faith, seems to have been superseded in favor of a different motivating context: reason itself as a meaningful instance. As a believing thinker, Anselm finds the meaning and motivation of his thinking not in the thinking itself, but in his faith. As a meaningful context, this traditional faith has primacy. Precisely to provide more credibility to this faith, and therefore to its meaning, he wants to determine the being of the object of his faith. Rational theology seems to seek to ask the same question but, at the same time, to omit Anselm's motivation.

People philosophize inspired by an orienting motive. This motive, that which motivates the thinking person, precedes the evidence and the thinking, just as a motive precedes its argument. Following Plato, it can therefore be said that the good, that-for-the-sake-of-which, the motive, is "on the other side of being." Thinking is motivated by that which is on the other side of being.

The question then arises: When philosophers try to think God, must he be thought as the highest being or must he be thought as the name that has been handed down to us by tradition? Thought on the basis of Scripture and tradition, is God a fundament of being? God is the motive; this motive is thought in philosophy as a fundament of being. God precedes this fundament of being in the order of knowing. Indeed, God is communicated by a tradition that makes him known. As a result, the question into the highest being, when it is motivated as a question of God, is not a final question. Why not? Because the question of how this highest being must be linked up again with God as the prior motive still remains. After all, the determination of God as the highest being, motivated on the basis of traditional faith, will have to link this interpretation of God back to the faith that has motivated it and has been handed down to it. This means also that philosophy as transcendentology can play a role in understanding God for the philosopher who wants to understand the God that has reached him by narratives. It plays an apologetic role.

On God as Meaning and Motive

Thinking and writing about meaning means thinking and writing about a difficult and almost impenetrable matter. It has almost the same dichotomy as we described with the words of Marion at the beginning of this article: The task of philosophy is to objectify, and with that it loses its object as a meaningful object: either it would be a question of phenomena that are objectively definable but lose their meaningful specificity, or it would be a question of phenomena that are specifically meaningful but cannot be described objectively. Nevertheless, I am not pessimistic about this dichotomy. The philosophical approach can be referred back to the original point of departure because we encounter the phenomenon of the hermeneutic circle when we ask about meaning (see Vedder). Questions about meaning suggest that there is already some prior knowledge of the subject being questioned. The question into meaning would not be possible without this prior understanding, and this prior understanding leads and orients further questions.

When an interpretation of God's being is given, the conclusion is already part of the premises, knowingly and deliberately. There is a deliberately confirmed or sought point of departure because that which is sought, God, is already known in a certain way. The point of departure of the interpretation will not change as a point of departure in the course of the interpretation, and will therefore also be the end of it. This is the circle as a concept in which beginning and ending mutually presuppose each other.

However, the question arises of how, within the hermeneutical circle, changes in insight can occur. How can a different view of this point of departure arise, and will the end then still be linked to this beginning in a discernible way? Will the point of departure remain the same or will it change? How does this point of departure relate to the interpretation that will be given to it in the course of time? Through the application and the interpretation, possibilities and meanings inherent in the point of departure become visible. This does not mean that the point of departure changes, but that it is made visible in all its richness. If I want to interpret something, the object that I interpret changes and appears to be different from what I thought. Stimulated by the interpretation of and comment on the word *God*, the issue of God calls for understanding. It calls for us to clarify the meaning and interpretation of that word. Thus, in an interpretation and a comment, an issue unfolds that is the origin. In the course of time, the issue yields a richer, and perhaps even unexpected, image concerning that first reference to the name of God that is the point of departure. This unfolding issue manifests itself in the impact of this first reference. The history of this effect, in other words, the history of the interpretation and its application, can become an independent object of study.

How does this effect relate to the hermeneutic circle? And how does the unexpected relate to the circle? The point of departure is enlarged and enriched in the interpretation. It proves to possess unforeseen opportunities or startling consequences. In the question of God, God reveals himself as the one who is; thinking about being reveals something about God as an entity who has being. In this hermeneutic circle, the interaction takes place between the issue or the person who asks for an interpretation and is interpreted, and the application of this very interpretation that refers back to the issue. Here, too, the issue is not so much the logical character of the circle, but the unfolding and interpretation of the point of departure—the being of God—and the concept of being that refers back to the being of God. The understanding of being, the experience of being, adjusts or enriches the understanding of the being of God.

Using this unfolding circle, it can be said that the meaning of the original statement develops in time. Time is an inexhaustible source of new insights and interpretations. Taking time seriously has consequences for the relation of the concept's content, on the one hand, and to the point of departure's reach, on the other. The original statement develops its unforeseen content in historical images. Nevertheless, these images are put into context and interpreted from the perspective of the original statement. That is how the hermeneutic circle works. However, when the point of departure becomes richer as it is interpreted and applied, this does not necessarily imply that it becomes more specified. An interpretation may wander from its point of departure or lose its way.[4] It may happen that the interpretation, although motivated by the initial issue, starts to lead a life of its own as the result of a pattern of thinking. In my opinion, this is the case in modern natural theology and in any pursuit in which the formal characteristics of meaning are perceived as the meaning itself. In natural theology this happens when the formal structure of meaning, or of transcendence, is perceived to be related to the Divine. This highest philosophical God is a formal God and is worshiped only by philosophers with their fascination for transcendence.

Here again we come to the notion of "transcendentology." As we see in Marlène Zarader's essay in this book, a great deal of philosophical discussion in France, and not only there, concerns the issue of transcendence. Against this background, Dominique Janicaud sees a theological turn in transcendentology, because, for Marion and Levinas, the notion of transcendence is linked with the notion of God as the Other. But what happens when the philosophical notion of transcendence becomes the framework within which religious meaning and the word *God* are made understandable? Then religion is reduced to a philosophical issue and has lost its specific religious meaning. It turns into an onto-theology (see Smith). However, Marion wants to avoid ontotheology because it robs the word *God* of its specific religious meaning. This brings us back to our original point of departure by way of an offer and a proposal of a philosophical insight.

When we speak of the rehabilitation of the original motive and point of departure, we do not mean to defend the claim that there is a pure point of departure rather than an interpretation or theory. A dogmatic position has the illusion that pure and robust points of departure can be determined. We do not observe unadulterated points of departure and pure motives. We read meanings that are part of and refer to other wholes of meaning. The texts and concepts in terms of which we think have always already been interpreted and are part of an interpretative history. This means that I am already absorbed by a meaningful horizon that codetermines what I read and understand and what I make the object of my thinking and interpretation. This insight also implies that I am always part of an ongoing tradition that has put its stamp upon me.

Interpretations cannot be separated from texts and concepts. Texts and concepts affect the interpretations. This effect, which is the issue here, is then thematized as an effect of a statement about God, an event in time and history. This effect can show that the text, the concept, or the document always contains more meaning than the original statement could have signified. The possible meaning emerges in the course of time. We could thus speak of a spectrum of meanings of a document, a text, or a motivating purpose. It also follows that one must already have the document within one's spectrum of interpretation to be able to understand it in some way. The fact that one already stands within the spectrum or effect of a document or concept, in this case the word *God*, means that the document or concept has previously touched and affected one; it is no longer entirely unfamiliar. A concept or text has already affected the person who wants to apply or understand it.

This fact also holds for academic research into scripture, the history of religions, and the philosophical reflection on transcendence and the being of God. Scripture, religion, and God as a motive of faith precede scholarly reflection on these subjects. This scholarly reflection has its own patterns and institutions. The effect of scripture and the accompanying determination of the image of God in Western culture have led, among other things, to the establishment of theological and philosophical disciplines which, in search of insight into the origin of the concept of God and the concept of being, can only be understood as an outcome of the texts, concepts, interpretations, and motives that are at their basis: the Bible and Greek philosophy as the motivating point of departure in thinking. Scholarly reflection concerning, and on the basis of, the concept of God is ultimately motivated by the effect that this concept has on Western culture and on making this culture what it is, something to which a scholar has always contributed. I therefore reject the distinction that is made between philosophical speaking "about God" and theology as an interpretation of faith and the effect of faith. Those who think it necessary to study God and the history of the concept of God exclusively in a philosophical way do so only by depending on and using a point of departure and a past the effect of which on themselves they deny (usually methodologically). However, they depend on their choice of an object of thought, because they were already part of the spectrum of meanings of the word *God* before they chose that object.

Metaphysical thinking about God is ultimately motivated by the wish to gain insight into the truth concerning God as it is presented in the religious texts that have been handed down to us in our context. In this activity, the things that we are searching for fascinate us. Thus, we are in the grip of that which we try to understand; it guides and orients our preunderstanding. The theoretical and academic approach that requires knowledge of, and insight

45

into, reality is also perceived as motivated by the question into the meaning of that which we refer to with the word *God*.

This implies that these thinkers know, or should want to know, who and what God is—in other words, that they have a theory about the transcendence and being of God, or at least that this is what they think about. Reflection tries to answer the question of what is meaningful and what is not, what is relevant and what is not, the object of reflection being the question of God. The process of understanding and unfolding interprets the truth of God; in its turn, the truth of God adjusts the interpretation. So the concept of transcendence receives ongoing correction from thinkers who are motivated by the issue of God. The interaction between issue and interpretation takes place within the hermeneutic circle. The interpretation of the issue of God is important to the extent that it teaches me to better understand the issue of God.

What matters to the interpreter in the relation between the interpretation and the issue is the very issue that has obtruded itself as the starting point of the reflection, or that has been chosen as such. There is more at stake than merely subjective representations; such shielding would preclude any adjustment. Therefore, what matters in scripture, in theology and philosophy, is not only the God of Abraham or God as the supreme being; what matters is God, knowledge about God. Insights into the issue of God, acquired in the application and interpretation of the point of departure, will provide adjusting feedback for this point of departure. The validity and tenability of the insights acquired and experienced in the pursuit of interpretation and gradual disclosure have an impact on that which emerges as the meaning of the point of departure.

This interaction between meaning and motivating point of departure is a process that develops in time. Through adjustment, renewed interpretation, and concrete application, the meaning of the name of God is unfolded in time. Time is an infinite source of new meanings and interpretations. The historical meaningful statement, or text, echoes through history to such an extent that it inspires literary, historical research. This echo of a not-yet-definitively fathomed meaning implies the necessity of time and history as a dimension in which this impact can work its effect. The definitive meaning of a statement cannot be determined precisely because of its ongoing historical effect, about which no one has spoken the final word.

The tempting thing about universal interpretation and reflection, however, is that it forgets the original, motivating word and allows reflection to become its own norm and criterion. This means that God is no longer the motive for thinking his specific transcendence. Instead, the philosophy of transcendence, transcendentology, becomes determined to understand God. In this, philosophy aims no longer at the issue that was the point of departure, but at itself. Philosophy is taken to be the situation that establishes the norms for thinking. Philosophy has thus gone its own way and lost its original point of departure, in this case the issue of God. With regard to the original word *God*, when philosophy goes its own way, God becomes a moment of being that must necessarily be thought; the intrinsic pattern of thinking establishes the norms concerning the issue of God, which means that the original point of departure is no longer the benchmark.

Especially in present-day culture, with its rational and efficiency-oriented attitude, the probability that thinking is no longer calibrated to the original experience of meaning seems great. On the other hand, when people experience something that touches and fascinates them, they discover that thinking fails. We are absorbed by what presents itself to us. The question seems justified of whether the philosophical approach to reality that focuses on understanding reality in our culture can in fact adequately deal with the phenomenon of meaning and meaningfulness. There seems to be no universal category for grief, loss, confusion, or the discovery of the unfamiliar. In a culture dominated by rationality, however, the most important thing is the representative (the inanimate), the quantitative (the numerical), the objective (the scientific), or the technically achievable. In a certain sense, everything is understood and experienced uniformly. This perspective puts the question into meaning in peril of disappearing. The question into meaning is thus perceived in terms of an effective ultimate object or destination, from which the purpose of life can subsequently be deduced. However, the human relation to meaning is not a functional relation that serves an ultimate goal, as if life can be understood as a professional occupation in which meaning functions as a reward or a retirement fund.[5]

Given the motivating point of departure, however, the principal question must be, What is a meaningful, valid effect here and what is not? Can we speak of a meaningful effect if the reflection has gone its own way? How do we know that we have remained true to the essence of the statement without losing sight of the point of departure? Which effect still belongs to the essence of the statement or concept and which is an arbitrary, subjective representation? The question of the validity and truth of meaning cannot be solved by leaving its fate to history. On the basis of what can we speak of a credible effect? When the question is the word *God*, is it safe to leave the validity of the effect to the intrinsic necessity of thinking? In my opinion, it is not. If it were, reflection itself would become the god of philosophy and reflection would be its own god; the issue of God would no longer be the point of departure.

Still, the pursuit of rationality in the statement "God exists" should not be perceived to be the original motive going completely off track. The fact that we pursue this statement rather than another should be regarded as one of the effects and an echo of the reverberating statement. On this level, the rationality developed here does not yield an experience of meaning on the basis of the original point of departure, but that does not prevent us from emphasizing the importance of rationality. The philosophical approach to the issue of God's being will have to be rational if it is to be taken seriously as a philosophical approach. This also means that other approaches are conceivable besides the philosophical ones—for example, poetical, narrative, pictorial, or musical approaches—and, like philosophy, all these can lose their original point of departure. Augustine pointed this out in his *Confessions*. He says that this is the case when someone is singing to praise the Lord, and then, while singing, forgets the praising of the Lord and begins to enjoy the pleasure (*concupiscentia carnis*) of the singing, the beauty of the tones and the songs (X.33–35).

God's Name of Being

We must conclude that the search for God and our talk about God always happens in the context of the stories circulating about him. Therefore, God is not to be had separately from that context: this means that he cannot be separated from a very concrete human tradition—from demonstrable and persistent attempts to discover meaning, coherence, and future. God cannot be isolated from the stories that are told about him.[6] The being of God is thus determined on the basis of a story—not any random story, but a story that inspires people. People want to live inspired by motives of meaning that really exist: determining the being of God is part of the story of God and not a separate thing. God is not handed down without being (see Marion, *God Without Being*.). Especially here the story provides us with the opportunity to ask questions about the reality and existence of God. A story becomes credible when it has a profound message for people. The philosophical approach to a story will ask questions about the reality of the story and, as a consequence, about what God actually is. This is where the question of the reality and being of God arises. An answer to this question is found on the basis of that which appears as a result of the issue itself and therefore on the basis of the indications that are provided by that very issue. Indeed, people who search for meaning will also ask about the reality and being of the meaning they seek; they will search for reality in, and on the basis of, that very meaning.

The thinking reflection that has evolved in philosophy in response to the story of God has understood and determined God as the essential and supreme being. The assessment of this, however, is not vested in the human being, or in the necessary pattern of thinking, but in God himself who has revealed himself. Therefore, we must ask what it means when God says of himself, "I am who I am" (Exodus 3:14). This is what God says when Moses asks for his name. (I wonder why Marion does not mention this Bible verse, though he mentions numerous other verses to make God understandable as love.[7]) The biblical God is handed down to us as the one who is; that is not only an onto-theological conclusion.

In the context described above, one can justifiably ask whether thinking about being answers the purpose of the person whose being has been revealed. The point is precisely that the question of God, including the question of transcendence and being, must be offered to God like a prayer. A God for whom a person can dance and pray will certainly also be a God about whom a person will be able to think. This is not a position that is situated outside the story and its effects. Time, history, and the story envelop and determine the concept of God. This is how it must be conceived, particularly against the background of this idea of the effect and development of a historical statement. Even the ahistorical definition of God can be understood as a development of the fact and the story of God's name. The question of whether this development is valid will be answered by the person whom the question is about. In this, the reflection will retain its openness to the revealed God. We cannot, after all, isolate an event from its impact and from the stories to which it gives rise. The history of God's name is part of its impact. An effect of this statement is that people have tried to understand its meaning, have begun to interpret the truth of this statement through "proof," and, moreover, have wanted to give definitions of God that hide him from the transience of the temporal. This effort would be unthinkable without the appeal that, prior to the effort to understand, motivates those who undertake to understand.

Against this background, the God of the philosophers cannot be understood without the God of the fathers. Often enough, the God of the philosophers is contrasted with Abraham's God as the God of the fathers. The juxtaposition of these two is an old tradition that should not necessarily lead to the separation of one from the other. In his comment on Exodus 3, Augustine already compares the name of God in verse 14 *"ego sum qui sum"* (I am who I am) with the God of the Fathers in verse 15. The first he calls *nomen incommutabilitatis* (a name of unchangeability), the second a *nomen misericordiae* (a name of mercy). Philo of Alexandria formulated a similar exegesis (see Runia, "God of the Philosophers" 15). In verse 14, God says that he is the existing one, which would mean that he does not really have a name. God as the existing one is impervious to the intellect. However, people are weak and they need a name; therefore God gives them the name of the three forefathers. Philo is seen as a representative of the movement in which biblical tradition was first linked with the philosophical thinking of Greek and Hellenist culture. This movement goes back to the translation of the Septuagint, in which the name of God is translated as "the Being one." In a way, the contrast arises from scripture itself, as God makes himself known to Moses in Exodus 3:14–15 by means of two names. The one seems to be the name for the philosophers, the other the name for the theologians.

Philo's contribution was that he regarded the Platonic paradigm as the most suitable philosophical system to interpret the truth revealed to Moses about God's living name, in which unchangeability is understood next to or in contrast with changeability. From this paradigm, it follows that God's first name refers to his unchangeability and to the fact that God is himself; the second name refers to origin, development, and changeability. Indeed, the patriarchs are temporal figures who appear in a history of which we ourselves are part. To what extent is there a contrast here between verses 14 and 15 of Exodus 3?

What has become clear in the above but has so far remained implicit and has not yet been discussed is that Exodus 3:14 has been translated differently over time. A changing understanding of being has had an effect on the translation of God's name. Philo understood that name by means of a Platonic paradigm, a paradigm that has a strong echo in Augustine's work. To them, the living name sounded like a preeminently appropriate appellation for God's transcendence. To them, the name "I am who I am" was Plato's designation for the transcendent reality that goes beyond the visible and changeable world. Augustine saw a direct link between Plato and Moses:

> But the most striking thing in this connection, and that which most of all inclines me almost to assent to the opinion that Plato was not ignorant of those writings, is the answer that was given to the question elicited from the Holy Moses when the words of God were conveyed to him by the angel, for when he asked what was the name of that God who was commanding him to go and deliver the Hebrew people out of Egypt, the answer was given: "I am who I am; and thou shalt say to the children of Israel, he who *is* sent me unto you"; as though compared with Him that truly *is*, because he is unchangeable, those things that have been created mutable, *are* not—a truth that Plato zealously held, and most diligently commended. (Augustine, *De civitate Dei*, VIII.11)

Scholastic theology follows the patristic tradition in interpreting and evaluating the living name in Exodus. Theologians such as Anselm, Bonaventure, and Meister Eckhart, to name a few, understand the name as a metaphysical determination of God's transcendence. Thomas Aquinas also unhesitatingly accepted the living name as the most appropriate name of God. The idea that the fusion of the Revelation and the Platonization of that which was revealed was not necessary, as is sometimes thought (e.g., Runia, "Platonisme"), seems to be based on a nonverifiable and nonattainable purity. The fact is that there was a fusion, and that the name of God cannot be separated from it. In fact, the name of God may be the key point in this fusion. In history, this fusion has had its own effect on the domains of theology and philosophy. However, this also means that, in this field, philosophy and theology are either the result or the victim of the same fusion in which the one cannot be isolated from the other. Such an isolation of the one will be unfair to the other, and vice versa. As a result, this fusion should be valued on its own terms. The God of the philosophers, therefore, cannot be separated from the God of the Bible. The names of God cannot theologically be separated. Indeed, what philosophy can distance itself from its historical and situational roots, the motivating and meaningful framework on the basis of which reflection takes place? The statements about God that have sparked reflection and interpretation are rooted in a tradition. The question of how God has entered into metaphysics does not need to be answered with the insight that God is an intrinsic moment in metaphysical thinking. A God who has revealed himself as the person who is, knocks at the door of philosophy and metaphysics. A philosophy or metaphysics that, on the basis of its own patterns, as an onto-theology or a transcendentology, keeps the door firmly locked, or says "You are already inside," is no longer able to listen to the original statement and remains deaf to what has already been said.

NOTES

1. Page numbers in brackets refer to the page numbers of the respective translations.

2. In my opinion, an important part of this discussion must be seen from the perspective of a changing self-image of philosophy as hermeneutics. Hermeneutic philosophy sees the human being, the world, and being as a text to be interpreted. Philosophizing takes place *more philologico*. One might even conjecture, in line with Albert, that the rise of the text model as a given to be interpreted goes back to the rise of the revelation model (131, 138). See Wilson, *Sein als Text*.

3. In using the word *motive*, I intend to avoid its psychological use. By *motive*, I understand that which inspires a person, that which pulls one forward. More or less, it is the motivational context, the Heideggerian *worumwillen* or *wozu*. It is not something that I have in my grasp; it attracts me only as long as I do not have it in my grasp.

4. Cf. De Boer, 136. De Boer says that the understanding becomes more specified.

5. I take the analogy from Sars and van Tongeren, 36.

6. "He is implicitly defined by these stories" (De Boer 148; my translation).

7. Cf. *God Without Being*, in which Marion mentions, for example, Romans 4:27 (86), 1 Corinthians 1:26–29 (89), Luke 15:12–32 (96), and Acts 17:28 (100).

WORKS CITED

Albert, Hans. *Traktat über kritische Vernunft*. 3rd ed. Tübingen: Mohr, 1975.

Anselm of Canterbury. *Proslogion, gevolgd door de discussie met Gaunilo*. Intro., trans., and annot. Carlos Steel. Bussum: Het Wereldvenster, 1981.

Augustine. *De civitate Dei*, VIII, chap. 11. Translation: *The City of God*. In *Great Books of the Western World*, vol. 18: *Augustine*, trans. Marcus Dods, 129–618. Chicago: Encyclopedia Britannica, 1952.

Burms, Arnold, and Herman De Dijn. *De rationaliteit en haar grenzen, kritiek en deconstructie*. Assen/Mastricht: Van Gorcum, 1986.

De Boer, Theo. *De God van de filosofen en de God van Pascal, Op het grensgebied van filosofie en theologie*. 's-Gravenhage: Meinema, 1989.

Heidegger, Martin. *Sein und Zeit*. Tübingen: Max Niemeyer, 1972. Translation: *Being and Time*. Trans. John Macquarrie and Edward Robinson. Oxford: Blackwell, 1990.

Marion, Jean-Luc. *God Without Being*. Trans. Thomas A. Carlson. Chicago: University of Chicago Press, 1991.

———. "Le phénomène saturé." In *Phénoménologie et théologie*, ed. Jean-François Courtine. Paris: Criterion, 1992, 79–128. Translation: "The Saturated Phenomenon," trans. Thomas A. Carlson. *Philosophy Today* 40, No. 1 (1996): 103–124.

Moors, Martin. "Het noemen van Gods naam: 'Hij Die is', over Filosofie en Openbaring." In M. Moors and J. van der Veken, eds., *Naar leeuweriken grijpen, Leuvense opstellen over metafysica*, 203–221. Leuven: Catholic University of Leuven Press, 1994.

Ben Vedder

Peperzak, Adriaan. *Zoeken naar zin, Proeven van Wijsbegeerte*. Kampen: Uitgeverij Kok Agora, 1990.

Runia, Douwe. "God of the Philosophers, God of the Patriarchs. Exegetical Backgrounds in Philo of Alexandria." In Van Reinier Munk and F. J. Hoogewoud, eds., *Joodse filosofie tussen rede en traditie*, 13–22. Kampen: Uitgeverij Kok Agora, 1993.

———. *Platonisme, Philonisme en het begin van het christelijke denken*. Utrecht: Department of Philosophy, Utrecht University Press, 1992.

Sars, Paul and Paul van Tongeren. *Zin en religie, wijsgerige en theologische reflecties rond de zinvraag*. Baarn: Ambo, 1990.

Smith, J. K. A. "Liberating Religion from Theology: Marion and Heidegger on the Possibility of a Phenomenology of Religion." *International Journal for the Philosophy of Religion* 46, No. 1 (1999): 17–33.

Steel, Carlos. "Inzicht en zingeving." *Tijdschrift voor filosofie* 49, No. 2 (1987): 297–307.

Vedder, Ben. *Erfgenamen van de toekomst, Heideggers vraag naar zijn als vraag naar zin*. Tilburg: Tilburg University Press, 1990.

Vroom, H. M. *De god van de filosofen en de god van de bijbel, Het christelijk Godsbeeld in discussie*. Zoetermeer: Meinema, 1991.

Wilson, Thomas J. *Sein als Text, Vom Textmodell als Martin Heideggers Denkmodell, Eine funktionalistische Interpretation*. Freiburg: Alber, 1981.

The Sense of Symbols as the Core of Religion

A Philosophical Approach to a Theological Debate

Paul Moyaert

In both philosophy of religion and theology, what makes a person receptive and open to religion is still an important question. With what interests and practices, traces of which can be found in a life not inspired by religious faith, does the religious life show affinities? The elucidation provided by this approach to religion can contribute to bringing religion in our time out of its isolation and back into the manifold forms of life that support and orient us.

In addition, this approach can contribute to helping all those who do not go through life as religious persons, and those who do not connect the significant events in their lives to religion, nevertheless to understand something of the point of religion. By "understand," I mean that they are able to recognize something in a life inspired by religion whereby that kind of life becomes less strange than it seemed at first. If you see nothing in the life led by a religious person, then you can understand that way of life only as something that alienates such a person from himself. When, on the other hand, you understand (in the sense of recognize) something about that form of life, then it refers to a way of life that is not simply foreign to you as an observer. It is then quite possible that the wonder which accompanies this recognition will precipitate a wonder about your own way of life, because something related to your own life appears in this recognition which, until that moment, you had no idea was connected to what a religious person does.

The answer to the question of a natural foundation for religion—natural in the sense of being grounded in what characterizes the human being as such—is intimately related to one's view of religion, or to the aspect of religion with which philosophers and theologians are concerned. But the converse is also true. Every definition of religion is related, explicitly or implicitly, to a view of the human condition.

One of the most important natural anchor points for philosophy is undoubtedly the human being's knowledge and love of the truth. According to this naturalistic approach to religion, both religion and science are products of one and the same striving for truth. In this view, religious belief is simply an extension of *believing that* something is the case. The core of religion is, then, centered on certain propositions that the believer takes to be true, and the reason that he or she takes them to be true is not fundamentally different from the reason a person would take scientifically supported ideas to be true. The content of these propositions can be considered on its own, without any significant loss of expressiveness, and this means that such content can be detached from particular rituals, concrete symbols, and traditional symbolic practices. This *abstract* content—abstract in the sense of detached from culturally determined external forms—can and should be submitted to the same critical demands as those that scientific rationality imposes on itself. In this view, then, it is important that people who exercise religious authority, who are partly responsible for the content of faith, maintain constant contact with changes and discoveries in science, since the "mysteries of the faith" must undergo continual adjustment to the latest scientific discoveries if they are to be rationally credible. As a result, this view assumes that a reasonably strict distinction can be made, within religion, between statements that must be understood in a literal sense and statements that can be understood only in a figurative sense. This distinction goes together with the assumption that form and content in religion can be separated from each other.

This brief outline of one approach to religion is beset by various difficulties. I will mention two of them. First, we do not tend to ascribe a religious sensibility to a person who is prepared to assent to the truth of faith only on purely rational grounds. A religious sensibility is strikingly similar to a poetic sensibility: you would not ascribe a poetic sensibility to a person who sees a poem as nothing but the expression of a content that can be separated from an apt choice of words and an elegant turn of phrase. Second, even if, in this view, one recognizes that belief (in the religious sense) is something other than knowledge, the view nevertheless emphasizes the importance of the believer knowing what he or she believes. Yet this overlooks the fact that knowing plays a radically different role in religion than in science. One could not say, for instance, that someone is a good scientist if he does not know the basic principles of science, whereas a person who is unable to accurately explain the basic tenets of his or her religion can still be an exemplary and pious believer.

It is well known that Karl Barth and the entire Reformation explicitly rejected this rationalistic approach to grounding religious faith. Knowledge of faith, *fides quae creditur*, is knowledge by faith, *fides qua creditur*. What one believes is religiously significant only in and through the act of faith—in other words, on the basis of an attitude that is already illuminated by faith.

By drawing on biblical exegesis of the word *faith* (*pistis*), a more existentially inspired interpretation will graft religious belief onto the fundamental attitude of basic trust. Here, a religious attitude is not explained in terms of "believing that," but in terms of "believing and trusting someone." The relation between faith as trust in God and various facts that can either support or undermine this trust should be understood by analogy with what it means in ordinary life to trust one another. A version of this view will refer to existential experiences in which notions such as receptivity, thankfulness for a generous gift, or participation in an atmosphere of love can be spontaneously brought about. Religion connects with this and expands the scope of these experiences by directing notions such as thankfulness, dependence, and dedicated love toward an infinite vanishing point that transcends the interpersonal human horizon and that is nevertheless addressed personally as God.

Though this discussion of the possible natural anchor points for religion is only a superficial overview, I limit myself to it because I want to examine a point that has been overlooked in many discussions in philosophy of religion: the capacity of human beings to understand symbols and carry out symbolic acts.

As far as Christianity is concerned, the view of religion that will be my guide here is expounded by those theologians for whom sacramental acts make up the core of the Christian profession of faith. From a theological viewpoint, the central role played by the sacraments in Christianity is supported by the basic mystery of the Christian faith: Christ's becoming human. The various sacraments are the continuation and expansion of this mystery. They encompass all the significant moments of human existence, from birth to death, and ensure that these moments are steeped in divine grace.

Christianity is an extremely complex religion, and this can be seen in the fact, among others, that the proper scope of sacramental acts was regularly the topic of theological debate. Theologians were often in disagreement about the significance of sacraments in experiencing one's faith. In the course of history, a notable theological debate evolved whose critical point was reached during the Council of Trent because that debate accentuated the already inevitable split between Catholic doctrine and what I here call the Reformation. This exceedingly complicated debate basically revolved around one aspect of the words pronounced by Christ at the Last Supper. During that dramatic celebration, Christ identified the bread and the wine with his body and blood. The words that he uttered have been called Christ's "instituting words" because through them he inaugurates the celebration of the Eucharist. In identifying himself with the bread and the wine, he renders himself present in these substitute signs. When the bread and wine are then sanctified in his name, he is once again actually present in the bread and wine that the faithful eat and drink. While contemporary phenomenologists of religion never tire of emphasizing that God is transcendent with respect to the acts and events by which he makes himself known to the faithful, a sacramental view of Christianity stresses that, despite his transcendence, God is *really present* in the sacramental acts carried out in his name.

Strictly speaking, what was at stake theologically in Christ's performative, meaning-instituting speech act was the "is" relation in *hoc* "est" *corpus meum*. That the celebration of the Eucharist constitutes the high point of Christian worship was not under discussion. The theological debate revolved entirely around a strong or a weak interpretation of the sacramental reality and symbolic efficacy of the Eucharist. Is it sufficient to conceive the "is" relation as a *sign relation*? Or do we also have to state and believe that, once consecrated, bread and wine are more than mere signs? It is a peculiar debate that comes across as strange and even laughable to outsiders. Does it not demonstrate how futile and ridiculous some theological arguments can become? Without getting directly involved in the labyrinth of scholastic theological distinctions, in what follows I would like to show what was at stake in this debate and demonstrate that what was at stake then is still relevant today for an understanding of religion.

My indirect approach to this theological debate will take the form of an examination of what characterizes a sense of symbols, specifically a sense of symbolic objects in a nonreligious context. In dealing respectfully with symbolic objects, a strong sensitivity to the incarnation of meaning plays a large role. I call this the "fetishistic character" of the experience of symbols. A close analysis of this character can, in my opinion, shed light on two significant dogmas, that of *praesentia realis* and that of *transsubstantiatio,* both of which were defended by the church fathers during the Council of Trent in relation to the Eucharist.

My oscillating between a phenomenological approach to symbols and a theological debate concerning the Eucharist is supported by the idea expressed at the beginning of this essay, which I summarize here: First, the sense of symbols forms the natural basis for a religious attitude. Second, a symbolic interest is an interest *sui generis.* It does not spring from other interests, such as a desire for knowledge, nor can it be reduced to other interests, such as an instrumental dealing with things. Third, the sense of symbols constitutes the very core of a religious attitude. This is related to the following considerations: in the view of religion by which I am guided, the essence of religion is about not orthodoxy but orthopraxy. This orthopraxy is not based on the acceptance of a belief that can be considered on its own, detached from symbolic practice, and subjected to rational criticism. Rather, the reverse is true: the confession of faith is itself a ritualized, elemental component of orthopraxy.

The fact that I can intervene in a theological debate from a phenomenological perspective implies that the discussions carried out at the Council of Trent were, indeed, not a purely theological affair. One cannot explain why Catholic doctrine and the Reformation gave a different meaning to the "is" relation in *hoc est corpus meum* by invoking fundamentally different christological views. As far as christological dogmas are concerned, these Christian currents were in broad agreement. What divided them, however, resulted from different views on the role and significance of symbols in religious practice. Catholic doctrine defends a view of religion that bears strong affinities with the experience of symbols in so-called primitive cultures. For the Reformation, on the other hand, the transmission of the message takes priority over symbolic practice.

Symbolic Objects

In his book *Meaning*, written with the help of his friend Harry Prosch, Michael Polanyi makes a simple distinction between signs as *indicators* and signs as *symbols* (70–75). He understands indicators to be transparent reference pointers, transparent because a person who is guided by them is neither explicitly nor focally directed toward them. In using the sign, we follow the direction that the sign indicates, and we concentrate on what the sign indicates or makes known. The sign itself is of subordinate importance because it is not the center of interest. Departing from the sign, we direct ourselves to a point that lies outside the sign itself. As examples of symbols, Polanyi mentions first of all nonlinguistic symbols, such as the country's flag, a medal, or the gravestone of someone we admire. In the case of symbols, the "from–to" relation is different than it is with indicators. What is of subordinate importance insofar as it denotes something else or stands for something else is at the same time an essential part of experiencing the symbol's meaning. The flag and the gravestone are parts of the symbolic process, parts that cannot stand on their own, but nevertheless they are *essential* components of what they symbolize. A symbol is not simply external to what it symbolizes; it is itself a part of what it symbolizes.

In this respect, the symbol is similar to a proper name. In his *Remarks on Frazer's* Golden Bough, Wittgenstein writes, "Why should it not be possible that a man's own name be sacred to him? Surely it is both the most important instrument given to him and also something like a piece of jewelry hung around his neck at birth" (4e). A proper name is more than an efficient means of reference. In a certain sense, it has grown up with its bearer to such an extent that it is also a part of the person. By blackening someone's name, we tarnish that person's reputation, and in playing word games with the name we attack the person himself or herself. Symbols function similarly to proper names. Just like a person's name, a nation's flag can be honored or abused. Whoever burns the flag will incur the wrath of the nation. In a symbolic relation, the two terms are not external to each other but interwoven. This intimate relationship is also characteristic of obscene words, as well as of everything that is sacred and holy in a culture. Obscene words are not just words that indicate something filthy; they are obscene in themselves. And holy things are not just things that are merely in a relation with something holy; they are holy in themselves. What is indicated by a symbol also affects the symbol itself. The signifying power of what symbols indicate penetrates into the symbol. In a symbolic relationship, the related terms flow into each other without completely overlapping or simply coinciding with each other. A symbol not only refers to something, it is also an *embodiment* of that to which it refers. One can more fully describe this interwovenness by saying both that the symbol is a component of what it symbolizes and that it partially contains what it expresses. The latter description can also be found in the dogma of *praesentia realis* (real presence): the consecrated host contains (*continet*) the body of Christ.

In the case of indication, the object of focal interest clearly lies outside the sign, and we can leave the sign behind as soon as it has achieved its goal. With symbolization, the focal interest is also brought to bear on the symbol, the bearer of meaning. Whereas the sign is destroyed as a pointer by explicitly concentrating on the sign, the symbol demands that one focus on the symbol. The symbol, then, is not merely a point of departure. In a certain sense it is also an endpoint. In the symbol, an "arrow loop" occurs, according to Polanyi (73), and by this he means that the "from–to" relation in the symbol follows a circular movement. Because symbols share the signifying power of what they indicate, I define them as embodied meanings.

Relics as Symbolic Objects

The phenomenon of embodied meaning is also emphatically present in a specific class of symbols not discussed by Polanyi: relics. It is well known that one can become emotionally attached to an object that belongs to a loved or admired person. Objects that are meaningful because of a demonstrable connection with a person or with a place where something important happened are called relics. In worshipping a relic, two dimensions of symbolic signifying power coalesce. On the one hand, a relic has the value of a sign, understood in a broad sense. It refers to something else and radiates a signifying power that captures the imagination. An entire world of meaning connected with the person or place is evoked. On the other hand, the beloved trinket is experienced as unique and irreplaceable, thereby falling outside the circuit of substitutable signs because the signifying power that it possesses cannot be detached from it and cannot be completely taken over by other signs. Even though one cannot see or feel the difference, an ersatz object does not have the same meaning. In this respect, interest in a relic is strongly similar to the interest of parents in their child. It is well known that parents may find it very important that the person they care for and to whom they are deeply attached really is their child. Now what makes a person *really* their child is inextricably connected with kinship ties, characteristics that you cannot feel and or see with the naked eye.

In the case of relics, just as with symbols in Polanyi's sense, *incarnans*—that which embodies meaning or, in passive terms, that which receives and supports meaning—and *incarnatum*—that which is embodied—flow into each other and are connected not extrinsically but intimately. The value of a relic is in no way due to itself alone. What the object is, how it looks, what it can be used for, or to what purpose it can be put—all this is of secondary importance. Its value is due to a material link or a relation of contiguity with a beloved person or place. In principle, anything whatsoever can become a relic as long as it has made contact with what is considered in some way to be important. An object that is elevated to the status of relic undergoes a *transformation of meaning*. For a relic, this transformation is dependent on a real, objective link with a person or place. When it turns out afterwards that this real link is absent, someone will be disappointed. The fact that great importance is attached to the presence of a real causal link in the symbolic practice of relic worship is comprehensible only on the basis of an attitude that is already sensitive to symbols. Detached from this perspective of a sensitivity to symbols, being touched by something is not a meaningful fact at all.

The phenomenon of meaning embodiment can also arise in a different way. This can be seen, for instance, in the case of a liturgical service in which objects that, until then, had an ordinary use-value acquire a symbolic value through being consecrated. That an object (the host, for example) is consecrated means that it becomes permeated with divine grace through the power of holy gestures and formulas. The transformation of meaning whereby an object is raised to the level of a consecrated object is expressed in a person's altered attitude toward this object. A son who is deeply attached to a relic of his father will carefully look after this symbolic object and touch it with respect. It will pain him to see that other people touch it in a nonchalant way. Believers will touch even the tiniest crumbs of the host, once it is consecrated, with great respect, just as the ashes of a deceased loved one (a relic) are treated piously. A transformation of the meaning of an object, whether by touching or by holy gestures and formulas, can indeed penetrate into the object's deepest fibers and smallest particles. The respectful attitude toward the *incarnans* that accompanies this transformation is an essential aspect of the *Faktum* of a practice sensitive to symbols, and this is what I call the fetishistic aspect of our dealings with symbols.

Embodied Meaning and the Rationalistic Theory of Symbols

By a rationalistic theory of symbols, I mean a theory that underestimates the importance of embodied meanings and tries to eliminate the fetishistic approach to symbols from the *Faktum* of symbolic practice. This theory does not take symbols to be a separate class of signs; it lumps signs and symbols in the same category. Like signs (indicators in Polanyi's sense), symbolic objects (relics, holy objects, etc.) are intended to bring a person into contact with a content. What counts, in this view, is that symbols bring to mind that which they stand in for as efficiently and clearly as possible. The important thing is that the signified, with the help of the sign, comes to mind as best it can. A rationalistic theory defines a symbol in terms of means-end categories and understands the means-end relationship as an external one. The intended goal lies outside the means with which the goal is attained.

If the point of departure of a rationalistic symbol theory is radically thought through, then it turns out that the symbol is, by definition, substitutable: the same idea can just as well be brought to mind by another means of communication. This conclusion, however, does not accord with the way that relics function. It is refuted by nothing less than the *Faktum* of symbolic practice—that is, by the way that people actually deal with symbols. Take, for instance, my dead father's cup which I use to drink my coffee. If we assume that this cup is significant to me only because it reminds me of my father and makes me think of something specific about him (the symbol reduced to a mnemonic), then I would have to be willing to replace the cup with some other, equally efficient mnemonic means without the slightest hesitation. But I do not do this. And because I do not do this, it follows that, for me, a meaning adheres to this cup in which this symbol, despite its sign value, is not fully assumed by its sign value. That the symbolic signifying power cannot be reduced to its sign value can be seen in the fact that the cup maintains a link with my father even at those moments when I am not thinking of him. *The symbol does something for me in my place*: it is a memento not merely in the sense that it reminds me not to forget about my father, but also in the sense that it remembers my father for me. The word "symbol" comes from the Greek *sumballein* and means: "to bring together, unite, bunch, gather." In honoring a symbol, the symbol maintains the link that it also created.

For me, drinking out of the same cup as my father drank out of means more than simply thinking of a certain content that is connected to him. The following examples illustrate the same phenomenon. You have undoubtedly seen the television images of people who are deeply moved by *touching* the names etched into the Vietnam monument in Washington. This touching of the *incarnans* (for instance, gliding softly over the letter with one's hand, kissing a crucifix or the photo of a loved one, drinking from one's father's cup, eating the host) can indeed have the poignant meaning of an intimate contact.

A rationalistic theory of symbols is wrong to claim that the *incarnans* is nothing more than an appropriate means of clearly and sharply evoking something that concerns a person. However, this incorrect interpretation also brings to light the peculiar role played by the *incarnans* in the *Faktum* of symbolic practice. I have already indicated that, for an attitude that is sensitive to symbols, it is essential that a symbolic object *really* did belong to someone or *really* was blessed. But the importance attached to this cannot be further described in terms of perceptions and mental representations. The fact that the object belonged to someone, or that it was consecrated, is an objective given, one that a person touching the *incarnans* cannot sense. And the importance of the real proximity of the *incarnans* cannot be explained by pointing out that this adds something essential to the mental content that the *incarnans* brings to mind.

That I touch a relic of my father, that this can deeply move me, and that I experience this touching as an intimate contact with my father does not need to be based on the *theoretical belief* that, in doing all this, I somehow re-establish contact with him through some bizarre science-fiction-like or surreal metaphysical channel. I do not have this belief, just as I do not believe that my dead father can read my thoughts about him or hear me when I pray to him at his grave. The significance of touching the *incarnans* is not a matter of magic or superstition, at least not when one construes magic as the ability, through touching or manipulating symbolic objects, to establish real contact with something or someone in a way that circumvents the objective laws of nature and that nevertheless produces a controllable and empirically observable effect.

An aspect of this is that a rationalistic theory of symbols can easily embarrass an attitude that is sensitive to symbols by demanding an explicit, rational explanation for the importance that a person attaches to the objective fact that the *incarnans* really did belong to someone or really was properly consecrated. Anyone tempted by the question of external rational justification risks having to seek refuge in an utterly implausible pseudoscientific theory or an illusory metaphysics.

If one accepts that embodied meaning is a crucial aspect of the *Faktum* of symbolic practice, one might wonder how the difference between symbols and nonsymbolic signs can best be described. As long as one is satisfied with determining this difference in a purely negative way (for example, symbolic objects are not merely substitutable signs, they do not merely stand for a content that can just as well be expressed in some other way), one can avoid concepts that would shock scientific reason and instrumental rationality. On the other hand, if one tries to determine what this being-more-than-merely-a-sign consists of, then one will have to reach for a somewhat unusual conceptual arsenal, one that runs counter to the sign structure: symbols are replete with and permeated with the reality to which they refer; they are full of the reality that is expressed in them; they are not only signs, they are also partially what they signify. For a nominalistic theory of signs, a theory closely related to a rationalistic view of symbols, these sorts of descriptions are hard to swallow. They will be seen as further confirmation of the suspicion that a symbolic consciousness is a confused consciousness, especially since this consciousness can apparently make no distinction between what someone thinks happens and what really happens. Subjective thought associations are confused with objective causal relations, so that what the mind links together is also projected onto the object pole. The mind thus confuses its thought associations with objective characteristics. This diagnosis also provides a psychological explanation of a consciousness that is sensitive to symbols: such a consciousness is a regression to an earlier stage of mental development, traces of which can also be found in children and in the mentality of what have been called primitive cultures.

But is it not overly simplistic to reduce the sense of symbols to a deficient capacity for making distinctions? An attitude that is sensitive to symbols— whether or not it is omnipresent, as in a primitive culture—has not lost all ability to make distinctions. In a primitive culture, not all fetishes are equivalent embodiments of the divinity, just as for a Christian believer not everything consecrated by the church radiates the same signifying power. A celebration of the Eucharist is worthy of greater respect than consecrating bicycles. And even if it is true that, in a primitive culture, the manifestation of divinity is always accompanied by an awareness of the real presence of the divinity, there is clearly still an ability to distinguish between the presence of the divinity in a fetish and its presence in forms such as dreams, visions, and other revelations. A son who honors a relic of his father certainly does not confuse this symbolically mediated presence with his father being present in real life. Even though the embodiment of meaning plays a role in various symbols, this does not necessarily mean that it always carries the same weight. However, all these distinctions are significant and comprehensible only on the basis of an acquaintance with the hierarchy of distinctions created by a symbolic order.

Instead of reducing the sense of symbols to a deficient capacity for making distinctions, why not interpret it from an awareness that the most powerful symbols form a separate class of signs? And why not interpret it simply as an attitude of respect for what is worthy of respect?

How can the analysis just carried out shed more light on the theological debate about Christ's instituting words?

The Dogma of *Praesentia Realis*

After prolonged and subtle discussion, the church fathers at Trent dogmatically laid down the following doctrine of the faith:

> If anyone denieth that in the sacrament of the most holy Eucharist are contained [*continet*] truly, really, and substantially, the body and blood together with the soul and divinity of our Lord Jesus Christ, and consequently the whole Christ; but saith that He is only [*tantum modo*] therein as in a sign [*esse in eo ut in signi*], or in figure, or virtue; let him be anathema. (Denziger 1651, can. 1)

This dogma consists of two parts: what must be rejected and what must be professed. From this dogma it is clear that the interpretation of the "is" relation in Christ's instituting words does not hinge on the alternative "sign vs. no sign." Instead, the discussion is about the necessity of stating that the symbols most worthy of respect for Christians—the sacramental symbols in the Eucharist—

are *both* signs and not *merely* signs. The dogma in no way denies that the eucharistic symbols fall into the general category of signs. First, the Tridentine dogma rejects the theological interpretation according to which bread and wine, in spite of having been consecrated, are no more than an extrinsic sign or a purely external indication of Christ's body and blood. The fundamental principles of a nominalistic theory of signs dictate that, in a symbolic sign, *incarnans* (signifier) and *incarnatum* (signified) remain external to each other. The categories of nominalism (*esse in eo ut in signi*) are unsuited to reflecting the interrelatedness of *incarnans* and *incarnatum*. Its symbol theory is too weak, hence incorrect. Second, the claim that the "is" relation should be conceived as a metaphorical, poetic figure of speech was condemned by the church fathers as being too superficial an interpretation.

What this dogma repudiates is a conception of symbols that corresponds to what I have called the rationalistic theory of symbols, the most extreme exponent of which, within theology, is Zwingli. He reduces the eucharistic symbols to *useful mnemonic signs*. For Zwingli, the holy Eucharist is important because it recalls the memory of a holy content. This throws open the door to what the phenomenologist of religion, Van der Leeuw, calls "the fatal pedagogical explanation of the sacrament" (247). Zwingli completely eliminates the mystery of the incarnation from the eucharistic celebration. This celebration is important only because it makes the believers think of something, and if this is the case, then the celebration of the Eucharist is reduced to a subsidiary matter, since the content can also be communicated through other channels. Both the church fathers at Trent and Luther were apprehensive about a Zwinglian evaporation of the symbolically incarnated mystery of the faith. For Luther, it is a diabolical desecration to claim that Christ's instituting words are only a matter of an extrinsic relation of meaning: "If the word 'is' means the same as the word 'indicates,' as Zwingli writes, and the phrase 'my body' means the same as the phrase 'a sign of my body,' as Oekolampad writes, then Christ's words would be, according to Zwingli, 'take, eat, this indicates my body,' and according to Oekolampad, 'take, eat, this is a sign of my body.' . . . I smell the devil in this."[1]

The Dogma of *Transsubstantiatio*

It was not so much the dogma of *praesentia realis* that was controversial, but that of *transsubstantiatio*. This dogma states the following:

> If any one saith, that, in the sacred and holy sacrament of the Eucharist, the substance of the bread and wine remains conjointly with the body and blood of our Lord Jesus Christ, and denieth that wonderful and singular conversion of the whole substance of the bread into the Body, and of the whole substance of the wine into the Blood—the species only of the bread and wine remaining—which conversion indeed the Catholic Church most aptly calls Transubstantiation; let him be anathema. (Denziger 1652, can. 2)

From my perspective on symbols, this dogma is more important than the dogma of *praesentia realis* because it also brings very clearly to light the problematic character of a *theologia rationalis*—that is, a theology that seeks a scientifically legitimate grounding for our sense of symbols.

It has been said that the term *transsubstantiatio* is highly appropriate for expressing something of the essence of the holy Eucharist. The dogma does not exclude the possibility that other words can just as well reflect the unique and mystery-laden event of the Eucharist, but the term is nevertheless well chosen because it fits Christ's performative speech act perfectly, better than terms such as *consubstantiatio* and *impanatio*. It is preferable to terms such as *transfiguration, transformation,* and *metamorphosis*, all of which indicate alterations that are directly visible to the naked eye. But neither the eye nor the mind can see any difference between the bread and wine before and after consecration, and while the external appearance or form of the bread and wine continues unchanged after consecration, the attitude of a believer who is sensitive to symbols has changed radically. I think there is even a third reason why this term is quite appropriate, a reason that is scarcely mentioned in the theological literature. The term *transsubstantiatio* is closely connected to the interplay of *meaning transformation* and *meaning embodiment* which is so characteristic of the fetishistic aspect of our experience of symbols. This interplay is expressed in the far-reaching change of attitude that the believer exhibits toward the objects that have been ritually consecrated and transformed into unique bearers of divine grace. Once they have been elevated to the status of symbols embodying divine grace, even the tiniest crumbs of bread and droplets of wine are treated with the utmost respect. This respect is not limited to those aspects of bread and wine in which one can clearly see a bread-like and a wine-like character.

This respect for the bread and wine is very similar to the respect accorded to a dead person's bodily remains, for even if one can no longer recognize a human shape in those remains, they are still not treated as ordinary material. Respect reaches beyond the visible presence of a human form; respect reaches also to the material substance that bears the features whereby something acquires a recognizably human form. In the Eucharist, this far-reaching respect comes to expression at the moment when the consecrated bread and wine are on the point of losing their recognizable form and no longer being edible and drinkable. When the bread and wine become spoiled, they are not simply thrown away like ordinary food scraps, but are disposed of with appropriate prayers and prescribed gestures.

That respect for the symbols of the Eucharist also concerns the very substance of those symbols—an aspect of worship that is directly connected to embodied meaning in a strong sense—was an important element in the debate between Rome and Luther. I believe that the importance of this is not emphasized enough in the theological literature (see Moyaert 148). In Luther's view, transubstantiation, or what he described as *consubstantiatio*, is at work only during the liturgical service—in other words, *in usu*. For Rome, on the other hand, *transsubstantiatio* is still at work *extra usum*. After the liturgical service, the most holy symbols do not revert to the level of *signa nuda*, or empty signs that can be filled with whatever meaning one wishes: once consecrated, always consecrated. An object does not lose its religiously laden meaning when it subsequently—after the service—is assumed into other contexts. It must be approached with the appropriate respect in whatever context it appears. This is why believers can also worship such an object outside the eucharistic celebration.

The phenomenon of embodied meaning that is characteristic of holy symbols goes together with the following: *everything holy is touchy*. What do I mean by this? When we say that a person is touchy, we mean that he or she is easily angered and somewhat irritable. A prickly person is quick to take offense and responds in an unsubtle and oversensitive (in the negative sense) way to what happens and to what others say. His or her responses are out of proportion to what the other person said. Someone who overreacts does not really take account of the circumstances (the context) in which something is said or the intentions underlying what is said. Words and gestures are taken out of context and burdened with a meaning that the agent in no way intended. It is hardly possible to deal in a neutral way with touchy people. We tend to approach them with a good deal of caution and keep a certain distance. In this way, we attempt to avoid a situation where our words and gestures, due to the physical proximity of a touchy person, acquire a meaning or connotation that we never intended. Unlike "touchy," the Dutch phrase "slightly inflammable" is applicable not only to persons and does not necessarily refer to negative responses in the moral sphere. Both notions share the idea of a reaction process that can be triggered by the slightest contact, without the object (what is touched) paying any attention to the question of whether such contact was intentional or not. Now, one could say that words, formulas, and everything holy are also touchy in precisely the same sense. The slightest touch of holy words and sacred objects can suffice to light the fuse and unleash something of the signifying power contained within them, regardless of the context in which the contact takes place and the intentions of the person who makes the contact. Holy things react to being touched in the same unsubtle manner that a touchy person does. The idea that the sacred and the touchy are closely linked is viable only for a theory of symbols that recognizes the importance of embodied meanings: a holy sign (a book, place, name, person, act, etc.) is not merely a sign that stands in relation to something considered to be holy; it is *itself* holy.

As an example, consider that the holiest symbols in any particular religion correspond to the name of God or the Divine. The word *God* is not only a name that refers to God; rather, God *is* his name. So it is not the case that this name sometimes does and sometimes does not refer to God, depending on the context or on the intentions of the person who pronounces this name. Even when this name is only being quoted, it must still be done with the required degree of respect. Believers may not take God's name in vain or use it wantonly, for this name is so *fused* with the reality it indicates that it defies the intentions of the user and also dominates the context in which it is said. Just by forming the name with one's lips, one touches God himself.

It is this aspect of holy symbols that is decisive for the scope given by theologians to the "is" relation of Christ's instituting words. When this scope is summarily restricted to the liturgical service itself (*in usu*), the path is cleared for a nominalistic view of symbols that minimizes the importance of embodied meanings. On the other hand, a theology that allows transubstantiation to work also in contexts outside the liturgy (*extra usum*) is a theology that stresses the importance of embodied meanings in the strong sense.

The term *transsubstantiatio* had already been circulating for some time in the speculative metaphysical discourse of scholastically trained theologians. Within that discourse, the term functioned not so much as an evocative description of what characterizes a symbolic practice based on a strong sensitivity to embodied meaning, but as referring to a real change in the symbolic objects, just like objective and real alterations in nature but situated at a deeper level of being, one lying underneath or behind the natural order of being, a level to which only speculative reason has access. *Transsubstantiatio*, then, functions not so much as a description of what is experienced as meaningful within the *Faktum* of symbolic practice, but as a theoretical justification of that practice. What is experienced as meaningful within the *Faktum* of symbolic practice is thus made to depend on ontological assumptions or presuppositions whose correctness must be resolved on a purely speculative level. In this way, the autonomy of the symbolic practice is put under immense pressure. If *transsubstantiatio* becomes the object of a speculative science (*theologia rationalis*), then theological thought must, of course, bend to the demands that scientific reason imposes on itself and investigate as accurately as possible how this extraordinary change of substance can be explained. If the elaboration of the theoretical presuppositions at the ontological (or metaphysical) level were to show that these presuppositions are untenable, or absurd, then in principle one would have to be willing to abandon the religiously inspired view of symbols that one was attempting to defend.

A minimal requirement of any rational discussion whatsoever is that one must always be prepared to pose additional questions that logically cohere with the questions that have already been answered, and to determine how these supplementary questions can be answered in light of the answers already provided. A second general requirement is that the endpoint of the series of questions is not established in advance.

Once rational discussion was set in motion, speculative theology found itself required to answer the following questions: How is it possible that uttering holy words can transform the underlying substance of bread and wine? How is it that precisely these and no other words can alter the substance of something? What actually happens to the invisible substance of the bread and wine? How does this substance disappear? Can the substance change without modifying the accidents that determine the external form? Can the *accidentia* continue to exist without a substantial change? How is such a thing conceivable within Aristotelian ontology? At what precise moment does the change take place—with the first word, after the second, or only at the end of the sentence? And in the case that *"hoc est corpus meum"* is not uttered in its entirety, does transubstantiation then get stuck halfway? If it takes place instantaneously, how can this be reconciled with the fact that various words must be spoken one after the other? Does the volume with which the words are spoken have any influence on the process? Why does the transformation occur when the words are spoken by a servant of God during a liturgical service but not when the same words are spoken in the theatre?

However strange the ingenious thought constructions of theology might appear, it is quite understandable that theology has brought all its imaginative and intellectual powers to bear in attempting to ground the sense of symbols in a rational theory of being. Through rational justification, theology tries to refute a psychological explanation of symbolic practice—in other words, one which says that a person's change of attitude (belief) with respect to holy objects is the result of a sort of conceptual confusion. It is indeed correct—so goes the argument of rational theology—that believers change their attitudes because there is a real change in the objects at the moment they are consecrated. It is not true that the believer who is sensitive to symbols is imagining things. Using the weapons of reason, rational theology also tries to oppose the increasing pressure exerted by a rationalistic view of symbols that, under the influence of the rise in modern scientific rationality, expounds a theory of symbols that is no longer supported by a strong feeling for embodied meanings.

The emphasis placed by rational theology on an ontological foundation for symbolic practice might also be related to the idea that the persons (believers) themselves also consider their practice to be dependent on the correctness of the thoughts that they associate with it. *Theologia rationalis* then assumes that these thoughts really do function for the believers as a theoretical foundation for their practice. However, when rational theology allows itself to be guided by this idea, it clearly overlooks the fact that the content of these thoughts does not necessarily function as a theoretical foundation of a person's practice.

However, by holding up *transsubstantiatio* as a dogma, the church fathers at Trent wanted to rescue this notion from the clutches of rational theology. They were attempting to avoid a situation in which *transsubstantiatio* would remain the object of a never-ending theoretical discussion, thus threatening, directly or indirectly, both the symbolic practice and the believers' peace of mind. For once *transsubstantiatio* has been assumed into dogma, the term no longer functions as an invitation to speculative reason to investigate the matter in a scientifically legitimate manner. The intention of rational theology was also to stop scientific curiosity about the mystery of the Eucharist. The dogma has a twofold aim: on the one hand, to save symbols from a disembodied rationalistic evaporation; on the other hand, to curb a certain kind of thinking about the Eucharist. In fixing the term dogmatically, an attempt was being made to incite theologians into transforming their *theologia rationalis* into a *theologia orans*. That this was indeed the concern of the church fathers can be seen from the explanation of the dogma in the catechism of the Council of Trent:

> According to the admonition so frequently repeated by the holy Fathers, the faithful are to be admonished against curious searching into the manner in which this change is effected. It defies the powers of conception; nor can we find any example of it in natural transmutations, or even in the very work of creation. That such a change takes place must be recognized by faith; how it takes place we must not curiously inquire. . . . Indeed, discussions of this kind should scarcely ever be entered upon. Should Christian charity, however, require a departure from this rule, the pastor should remember first of all to prepare and fortify his hearers by reminding them that no word shall be impossible with God (Luke I, 37). (*Canons and Decrees* sec. 43)

Guided by the idea that the symbols most worthy of respect form a separate class of signs, the dogma permits one to investigate whether the term *transsubstantiatio* reflects, better than other terms, the essence of the difference between strongly embodied symbolic meanings and weakly embodied signs. At the same time, however, the dogma wants to protect a truth of the faith that is anchored in symbolic practice and place it at a distance by removing it from the curiosity of speculative reason. The dogma is a prohibition and has something of a taboo about it: it demands that it be respected and honored, and prohibits anyone from touching it or from unhesitatingly penetrating it with reason. Just as words that directly indicate a taboo (obscene or holy) are themselves taboo, so the dogma is a direct embodiment of what is holy.

Balance between Literal and Figurative

A Roman Catholic view of religion argues in favor of taking symbols seriously. Taking symbols seriously, submitting to them, and being religiously touched by them is not the same as interpreting them literally. However, one would threaten the seriousness of symbols by simply adding, with no further explanation, that one should not construe them literally. To keep the seriousness of symbols from having its meaning hollowed out and also from a rationalistic evaporation of the *incarnans*, the Council of Trent stressed the importance and the necessity of a literal interpretation of the dogma. On the other hand, it is clear that a certain conception of literalness stifles the sense of symbols, namely the conception which states that what can only be understood from an attitude that is sensitive to symbols possesses the same kind of literalness as the one aimed at by the rational ontology of a scientific discourse whose objective truth does not depend on the symbolic practice. Taking symbols seriously is then made to depend on the correctness of epistemological insights and hypotheses, thereby overlooking the sense of symbols as an *ordo sui generis*. In order to avoid the undesirable consequences of literal or physicalistic interpretation, one tends to neutralize this interpretation by adding to it the qualifier "as if."

To take symbols seriously is to strike a balance between accepting and, at the same time, rejecting two extremes. Looked at on its own, each extreme is either too strong or too weak, and to affirm both simultaneously is hardly a comfortable position. People asked to justify their sense of symbols are immediately embarrassed, for as soon as they try to meet this challenge, they are no longer sure what to say: neither literally nor figuratively, or both literally and figuratively. Symbols are signs that are not merely signs, without thereby ceasing to be signs.

NOTE

1. Cited in Van der Leeuw 77. For a more detailed determination of the positions of the most prominent Reformation thinkers on the subject of the instituting words and the Catholic doctrine, see my book, *De mateloosheid van het christendom*.

WORKS CITED

The Canons and Decrees of the Sacred and Oecumenical Council of Trent, Celebrated under the Sovereign Pontiffs Paul III, Julius III and Pius IV. Trans. Rev. J. Waterworth. To Which are Prefixed Essays on the External and Internal History of the Council. London: Burns and Oates, 1848.

Denziger, Heinrich. *Enchiridion Symbolorum: Definitionum et Declarationum de Rebus Fidei et Morum.* 30th ed. Ed. P. Hünerman. Freiburg im Breisgau: Herder, 1999.

Moyaert, Paul. *De mateloosheid van het christendom.* Nijmegen: SUN, 1999.

Polanyi, Michael, and Harry Prosch. *Meaning.* Chicago: University of Chicago Press, 1975.

Van der Leeuw, Gerard. *Sacramentstheologie.* Nijkerk: Gallenbach, 1949.

Wittgenstein, Ludwig. *Remarks on Frazer's* Golden Bough. Trans. A. C. Miles. Ed. Rush Rhees. Retford: Brynmill, 1979.

Philosophy and Transcendence

Religion and the Possibility of Justice

James E. Faulconer

Real justice must be particular. It must always occur within a specific, historical community with specific norms, beliefs, customs, forms of expression, and so on. Without that historical specificity, justice can be no more than abstract justice for abstract people. On the other hand, the particularity of justice leads to injustice; without the concept of justice and its concrete forms, we will be unjust. The very norms and customs required for justice to be concrete are always a threat to justice because, at the same time that they make justice possible, they can be the means for doing injustice. In fact, they are probably most often the source of injustice: we use traditional norms, beliefs, and customs to justify excluding or persecuting those who do not stand under the umbrella of those norms, beliefs, and customs.

The most obvious solution to this problem is an appeal to transcendence of some kind, to something prior to or fundamental to every set of historical conditions and norms, making those conditions and norms possible. The question is how to do so. For historical, philosophical, and political reasons, reasons that overlap, few are nowadays willing to appeal to God for the transcendence needed. Since the sixteenth century, such arguments have been less and less acceptable. For philosophers, they are difficult to make given the kinds of basic assumptions from which modern and contemporary philosophers are willing to begin. At the practical level, there is sufficient divergence of understanding of God among the citizens of any contemporary, working democracy—from solid belief, to agnosticism, to atheism—that it would be impossible to make an appeal to divine transcendence. Even among those who are religious there is sufficient difference in the understanding of the Divine that it is not clear that any particular appeal to divine transcendence would be effective. But if the appeal to divine transcendence will not work, what about an appeal to transcendence of some other kind? The problem remains the same: it is not the word *God* that is the problem; it is transcendence and our seeming inability to have access to anything transcendent. In the face of this inability, what can we do?

Kant gives us one appealing and now common answer. He recognizes the need for transcendence in recognizing that all human judgments are situated in historical contexts but that justice demands that we go beyond those contexts. As a religious person, part of my context is my religious beliefs.[1] But if others' beliefs about religion differ sufficiently from mine, then I cannot understand their position in order to respond to it reasonably if I merely assume that they are wrong and I am right. Even if I strongly believe that I am right, if I am to deal with them justly, I must exercise the principle of charity and find a way to grant the possibility that their position is right. Not to do so is not to understand them and, so, not to be charitable.[2]

This creates a dilemma. As the first *Critique* shows, I cannot use reason alone to make claims about transcendent matters, so I cannot use it to decide moral questions. Such claims necessarily occur within the particularity of a history and tradition and, so, cannot be made "purely." However, morality (among other things) *requires* that I be able to go beyond such local, particular claims. Kant's solution to this dilemma, a dilemma of how to appeal to what transcends the particular without appealing to a world to which I have no rational access, is to recognize the other person as orienting himself or herself in the world differently than I do, sometimes quite differently. Since my understanding of the world is, to me, quite reasonable, I must recognize that there is something alien about the other person's understanding of the world and I must accept the *possibility* of that orientation, even if I do not accept its truth. Morality requires the principle of charity; in other words, it requires that I assume that I could be wrong, even if I do not know how I could be. The transcendence needed for justice is also found in the principle of charity. The question is how it is possible to exercise the principle of charity.[3]

One answer is to assume that the other is like myself: by the power of imagination, I can envision what the other needs or desires and, based on that, I can put myself in his or her place. In other words, the Golden Rule. However, the Golden Rule will not work. In the first place, it requires that reciprocity be possible between the other and me. In the question of justice, however, that is often the very question at issue: Is reciprocity possible? Can I use the judgments that I would make of myself in a particular case to decide what my behavior should be with regard to the other person? If the other person requires or asks something that is completely different than I understand the good to be, by what reciprocal measure is it possible to measure that request?

Reciprocity will not allow for such a measure, for in a reciprocal relation, I can think only in terms of identity: The other person is like me, of the same genus; if I understand our relations in terms of our sameness, we are each only a place holder in a genus identified by a set of characteristics and, therefore, our relation is, at best, merely bilateral. To use Paul Ricoeur's terms, the person in a reciprocal relation can recognize the other as *idem*, but not *ipse*—as identical in characteristics, but not "the same" in having a personal identity and, therefore, in being different, in being other. In reciprocity, the other person is always, at best, another me.[4] Thus, contrary to the usual assumption, I do not think that the principle of charity can be understood if it means that we simply assume that we are like one another. I cannot take into account the strange claims and strange reason of the other person by theoretically putting myself in the other person's position. Thought of as the Golden Rule, the principle of charity begs the question.

However, even if reciprocity were possible, the Golden Rule would not work. Without complete self-transparency, nothing checks the projection of skewed or perverse desires onto the other person. I cannot guarantee that my self-knowledge is accurate, that I am not self-deceived or misunderstanding myself in some way. I cannot guarantee that my understanding of my desires is not perverted. I cannot guarantee my own good will. But if my will is not good, then when I project my desires onto another person, I may well do what is unjust rather than what is just. The Golden Rule is insufficient because I cannot trust my self-understanding to tell me what justice demands. I may be wrong about what I would that others should do to me. In a relation of reciprocity, I can recognize the other person as like me (though perhaps only perversely), but the other person's difference remains merely incomprehensible and, so, irrelevant. Of course, for difference to be comprehended would be for it to cease to be difference. However, if it remains merely incomprehensible, then it cannot be taken into account in any search for justice. Personal difference, sexual difference, national and ethnic difference—all such differences are extraneous to a reciprocal relation, though at some points justice demands that the person be recognized as an individual, which always includes such differences.[5] Though fundamental differences must remain, strictly speaking, incomprehensible, justice requires that they be taken into account. How is that possible?

The question of justice is, unavoidably, the question of transcendence: If I cannot step outside of my context and experience to learn a universal law or to partake purely in universal reason, how can I make decisions about another that are just, on the one hand, and how do I avoid sinking into mere cultural relativity, on the other? What transcends my subjectivity and allows me to relate to someone other than myself?

I do not propose to answer that question directly or fully. However, I do propose to show something of what biblical religions might say in response. I will look briefly at the biblical story of Moses and Israel to examine what we can understand it to say about transcendence and what that might mean with regard to the question of justice. In referring to this biblical story, I am not moving from philosophy to theology. Rather, I am looking at the sacred text of a loosely related group of historical communities and assuming that it may have something to say to us about how we can understand the transcendence that makes justice possible. Biblical religions have considered the problem of justice and have responded to it with understandings of human existence that can provide us with possibilities for consideration.

The usual assumption is that the transcendence that we find in religion is otherworldly transcendence. However, for the most part, that is an assumption, and often not a well-founded one. (I will take up that hedge, "for the most part," after my reading of the story.) As Michel Henry has pointed out, our understanding of what religions say about transcendence is often rooted more in a circulating set of uncritical assumptions than in the texts of religion.[6]

My claim will be that the community we find in the Old Testament, in the story of Moses and Israel and in other stories, does appeal to transcendence as a means of overcoming the problem of justice. Nevertheless, this appeal does not have the character that we often suppose. The story of Moses and Israel does not merely invoke a notion of transcendence as radically outside of or other than this world. As shorthand, we might say that biblical understanding of transcendence is not Greek. However, the transcendence that the text invokes, religious transcendence, remains problematic. In fact, it is transcendent in being problematic, in being a break in history and the human world that requires constant recuperation. I will argue that the biblical story of Moses and Israel shows us two kinds of transcendence. First, it shows us historical transcendence: We always find ourselves in a context that we are given and that constitutes us, an origin that is not of our making. We also find ourselves directed toward some concrete end, an understanding of how things will be that motivates what we do and establishes who we are. Like our history, this orientation toward the future—a point of origination as much as is the past—is not of our making. Past and future make us. Concrete past and future— together a determinate origin that is incapable of final determination, so always giving rise to new meanings and possibilities—are transcendent and our relation to them is transcendence. Our origin constantly draws us beyond ourselves and constitutes us in doing so. However, second, this historical origin is not the only kind of transcendence, for in it we find interruption, the interruption that makes the determinate origin also indeterminate. Our origin is broken, incapable of final determination, so it always draws us beyond not only ourselves but also beyond our historical context and constitution.

Israel thinks transcendence *in* rather than *of* history. My reading of the story of Moses and Israel is intended to show how we can understand that transcendence in history:[7] a historical origin that is, nevertheless, always disrupted by something that it cannot account for, something ahistorical; a historical destiny that always remains promised, that is not achieved in history. Contrary to what we might expect, this origin and this destiny are marked by breaks and gaps in the story rather than by the revelation of some ahistorical transcendent thing or person. Moses' personal encounter with God at the burning bush is marked repeatedly with a rejection of his question of what God is like. I think the same thing can be said of his encounter with God in Sinai on behalf of Israel. So, Israel is not founded on the revelation of what is outside of history in its beginning or on that which it aims for outside of history in the end. Israel is founded on its historical origin and its aim (the Abrahamic promise), but that origin and that aim, though both are specific and concrete, are also disrupted, so they cannot be reduced to their content. The being of Israel can be neither reduced to a specific content nor separated from a specific content.

Consider an overview of the story that I will examine. It begins in Genesis 37 with jealousy between Joseph and his brothers, the sons of Jacob (who is now called Israel). Joseph's brothers sell him into slavery and he winds up in Egypt. There he prospers and becomes a minister of the pharaoh. Because of a famine in Israel, his brothers must come to Egypt for grain. Joseph and his brothers are reconciled, and the family moves to Egypt, under Joseph's protection (Genesis 41–47). Years later, after Joseph and his brothers are dead, a new pharaoh enslaves the Hebrew people, collectively called "the children of Israel," because he is afraid that the Israelites will outnumber the Egyptians and take control of Egypt. When enslavement does not reduce the number of Hebrews, the pharaoh orders the Hebrew midwives to kill all male children at birth, though the midwives disobey him by subterfuge. He then orders his people to kill the Hebrew male babies (Exodus 1:8–22). When Moses is born, his mother hides him for three months, but when she can no longer hide him, she makes a basket of bulrushes, and she puts Moses in the basket at a place on the river where he will be found. She leaves Moses' sister, Miriam, to see what happens (Exodus 2:1–10). The pharaoh's daughter discovers the baby and pities him. Seeing Miriam, she asks her to fetch a Hebrew nurse for the child, and, of course, Miriam gets her mother. The Egyptian princess adopts Moses (Exodus 2:11–15). As an adult, Moses sees an Egyptian taskmaster beating a Hebrew slave. He kills the taskmaster and hides the body. The next day, however, another Hebrew mentions the killing to him. He has been discovered. The pharaoh finds out about the killing, so Moses flees Egypt, going into the desert to Midian (Exodus 1:15–17). At a well in Midian, Moses meets the daughters of Jethro, and he helps them water their flocks. Jethro invites Moses to live with him, and Moses marries one of his daughters, Zipporah (Exodus 2:18–22). While tending Jethro's flocks, Moses comes upon a burning bush, from which God speaks to him, commanding him to return and lead the children of Israel out of Egypt (Exodus 3:1–4:23). Moses returns, but at an inn on the way, God tries to kill him because Moses has not circumcised his son. Zipporah performs the ritual, saving Moses (Exodus 4:24–26). In Egypt, the pharaoh is unwilling to let the children of Israel go free. In fact, in response to Moses' demand, he increases their workload (Exodus 5). God sends plagues on the Egyptians, plagues that culminate in the death of all the firstborn in houses that have not put ritual blood on their doors (Exodus 7:15–12:30). With that final plague, the pharaoh relents and allows the Israelites to leave, but he changes his mind after they have gone and pursues them with his army. At the Red Sea, the waters part miraculously, allowing the Israelites to cross over, but drowning the pharaonic army when it follows (Exodus 12:30–14:31). The Israelites go to Mount Sinai where, through Moses, they covenant to be God's people and receive the Mosaic Law (Exodus 19 ff.). They wander in the desert for forty years, vacillating between fealty to the covenant and the desire to return to the plenty of Egypt (see, for example, Numbers 11:4–5). At God's command and in response to one of Israel's complaints, Moses brings water from a rock (Numbers 20:7–11). However, when he does so, he takes credit for the water, making himself equal to God (Numbers 20:10). Moses' punishment is that he will be allowed to see the Promised Land, but not to enter it (Numbers 20:12). Under Joshua's leadership, the Israelites cross the Jordan River miraculously, repeating the miracle of the Red Sea, and enter the Promised Land. They begin to kill those already living there, the Canaanites, and they establish the nation of Israel (Joshua 1 ff.; see especially chapter 7 and 13:13).

The story of Moses and Israel is rich, and a good deal could be said about the understanding of human beings that one finds in it and in other biblical texts. Consider, however, only one detail: the way that the text structures the life of the individual, Moses, and the community, Israel. First consider the chiasmic structure of Moses's life:

A. Moses is born into Israel.
    B. Moses is cast out of Israel by the violence of the pharaoh, who demands the death of all Israelite males.
        C. Saved by the pharaoh's daughter, Moses lives as both Egyptian and Israelite, though primarily the former.
    B'. Moses is cast out of Israel when he kills an Egyptian taskmaster for beating an Israelite and is betrayed by an Israelite.
        D. Moses wanders in the desert.
            E. The epiphany on the mountain: God appears in a burning bush.
        D'. Moses wanders in the desert.
    B''. Moses enters Egypt attended by the violence of his son's circumcision. Because he has neglected to perform the circumcision, God tries to kill him; only the intervention of his wife, Zipporah, saves him.

C′. Moses lives in Egypt with unusual access to the Egyptian court—in other words, as both Egyptian and Israelite, though primarily the latter.

B‴. Moses leaves Egypt with Israel after the deaths of Egypt's firstborn.

A′. Moses should be "born" into the new land of Israel, but he is not. He dies, not allowed to enter the land.

The center of this chiasmus is a point of disruption and covenant, around which the rest of Moses' life turns. The origin of Moses' life is found in its center, in his experience with the burning bush on the mountain, where the horizon of history is disrupted by the vertical. However, the content of this disruption and origin is anything but clear. Before the burning bush, Moses' first question is, "Who am I?" (Exodus 3:11). But the Divine does not answer this question directly. Rather, he promises, "I will be with thee" (Exodus 3:12). Moses asks for a determination of self. Instead, God promises to accompany him. In a relation where reciprocity is impossible, Moses is moved beyond determination. Moses is given who he is by being accompanied by the non-historical. Because the nonhistorical is not a being within the world and the limits of history, it is not with Moses as one being is beside another. Such a side-by-side relation is either no relation at all, like the "relation" between the table and the chair, or it is a matter of mere reciprocity, an exchange between identicals. Instead, Moses is the being called to labor in an event that disrupts history in a quest for justice. Moses is Moses by being called to a labor, by being one "drawn out" (Exodus 2:10), by being one whom God is with. The disruption of history by this alterity is also a disruption in Moses' being; the trace of "what is" beyond history is within Moses, making him who he is. What he is, however, remains to be determined in the labor for justice to which God has called him, and God remains with Moses in that labor and in Moses' indetermination.

Similarly, when Moses asks about the name of God, he gets no answer. God, too, remains indeterminate. The King James translation of the text gives us God's reply fairly literally as "I am that I am" (Exodus 3:14). According to the medieval commentator Nachmanides, it means, "As you are with me, so I am with you" (36).[8] In Nachmanides' reading, when Moses asks "Who am I?" the Divine responds, "I will be with you." Now, in answer to the question "Who are you?" God says, "As you are with me, so I am with you." If Moses' origin is traced in his being by the disruption of the nonhistorical, what does it mean to say that the being of the nonhistorical is given by the being of the individual? Perhaps that we find the nonhistorical only in the historical. It is not *the* Revelation, but *a* revelation. The story does not appeal to the one word that can be said, the one thing that can be seen. Instead, it shows us that the word must be continually reappropriated: continuing revelation rather than revelation once-and-for-all.

We can apply what we see in this relation between God and Moses to the community. God is not determined by his attributes, though he has them; as a person, he is and is not a this or a that. There is no merely determinate answer to the question "Who are you?" but there is an answer, and it is also not merely indeterminate. The origin is always something, but never only something. There are two ways to think about the origin of a community: one can suppress either the determinate or the indeterminate. On the one hand, we can ignore the indeterminate and decide the origin of community, making this determinate origin our beginning. We see this approach to origins in racism and nationalism. On the other, we can overlook the determinate and decide that there is no origin, nothing that disrupts history, an approach that we see in historicism and in some of what passes for postmodernism but that I think can more accurately be called hypermodernism. Both do justice neither to the origin nor to persons. Moses finds discontinuity in himself and otherness in God. God is other than his determinations, but determined—predicated *and* prior to predication. As one who is in God's image, so is Moses and so is Israel.

Perhaps surprisingly, we see a reflection of the chiasmus that structures Moses's life in the structure of the history of Israel, though the chiasmic structure of the latter is incomplete:

A. Israel the person is born.
> B. Israel the nation enters into Egypt through the violence between Joseph and his brothers.
>> C. In Egypt, Israel is both Israelite and Egyptian, though the latter is dominant.
> B'. Through the death of the firstborn sons of Egypt, Israel leaves Egypt.
>> D. Israel wanders in the desert.
>>> E. Moses has an epiphany on the mountain.
>> D'. Israel wanders in the desert.
> B". Israel enters the Promised Land, slaying the Caananites.
>> C'. Israel lives as both Israelite and Caananite, though primarily the former.
> B'''. . . .

A' . . . .

Comparison of this chiasmus with the previous one shows their parallel structure. Just as Israel is the microcosm of the world, Moses is the microcosm of Israel. As the rabbis might say, the lesser is the figure of the greater. The nation of Israel is born in the person of the twelve sons of Jacob. Because of strife between Joseph and his brothers, Israel moves into Egypt. While in Egypt, Israel is both Egyptian and Israelite, just as Moses was both Egyptian and Israelite, and, just as with Moses, being Egyptian is primary. Then, through the events of the Passover, this dual existence ends when Israel is "cast out" of Egyptian bondage into the wilderness.

As was true for Moses, the turning point of this chiasmus is the disruption by the Divine at the mount. For Israel, this is disruption of covenant, a covenant that, as Emmanuel Levinas points out, has the recognition of those on the margins at its communal center: the stranger, the widow, and the fatherless define the communal relation (190 [215]).[9] At Sinai, the community of Israel gains an origin, an origin explicitly found in recognizing those on the margins, in being called to justice for and by those who are indeterminate for the determinate community. At Sinai, Moses meets with God again, only this time he is no mere individual. This time he is an individual in relation to another (at least God), and he is laboring for the Other and for the members of the nation of Israel. From the mount, Israel returns to the wilderness and, finally, enters the Promised Land—where the Israelites begin to destroy the inhabitants of the land.

After entering the Promised Land, the chiasmus for Israel breaks down. It has no closing corresponding to the closing in the chiasmus of Moses' life—though since Moses was forbidden to enter the Promised Land, the closing of his life is also not a closing. As does the second chiasmus, apocalyptic literature anticipates the close of the chiasmus of Israel, and it anticipates the violence that marks that close, violence parallel to the strife between Joseph and his brothers. But apocalyptic literature only anticipates that close. The apocalypse is irrecuperable.[10] The Just Kingdom remains hidden; its revelation always remains awaited. Pure Israel, without margins or remainder, without not only the priests and the Law, but also the strangers in the Promised Land, is impossible. We cannot understand the Law and the strangers apart from each other.[11] The strangers point beyond what one expects to see at the margins, for the strangers in the Promised Land include not only the widows and the fatherless who, Levinas reminds us, are at the heart of Israel's existence, but also the enemy, those whom Israel destroys. The second chiasmus suggests that, in history, there can be no pure Israel—except in covenant memory and apocalyptic hope. The purity of Israel is to be found in its memory of its beginning and its hope for justice, not in any possible present situation. Supposed communities that forget this and insist on completion (naming their origin as something fully found or revealed, at hand and fully explicable, within themselves) or on denying all ground and excluding its possibility (naming their origin as merely indeterminate or as absent) will be unjust. Communities that insist on their purity, whether pure affirmation or pure skepticism of affirmations, are necessarily unjust. By deciding their origin—as either fullness or absence of content—they refuse the ground that makes them possible.

The labor of the community is the labor to bring about the just community—hopeful labor. Thus, the incompleteness of this chiasmus points to the necessary historical impossibility of finishing the labor for justice. The incomplete chiasmus shows that the hope that drives the labor for justice is unfulfillable. It is historical hope for the end of history. In other words, it is faith. Since it is a concomitant of labor, true community is always under way toward justice and in danger of annihilation. One must labor to complete the just community, then, though we cannot complete it in time (in both senses of the term "in time"). However, because community only occurs in the labor for justice, in the labor to complete the community, it is also always in danger of disappearing. To believe that one has reached the end of history is to believe that the labor for justice is finished. It is, therefore, to destroy the possibility of human justice, a justice defined by its labor rather than by the particular state that it achieves.

The incompleteness or undecidability that structures the history of Israel is not the only incompleteness. The absence of Moses' death in the first chiasmus suggests that just as the community is not completed, Moses' life is also not completed. Because the community cannot be completed, Moses cannot enter the Promised Land. (In a sense, Israel also enters it without entering.) Within Moses, too, are the seeds of collectivity, for in taking credit for providing the Israelites with water, Moses denied the divine interruption of his individuality (Numbers 20:7–12).[12] He defined his origin, and he defined it as himself. At that point, Moses ceased to labor for the just community, a labor that is the site of both individuality and relation. Deciding the origin, he lapsed back into mere autonomy. Moses forgot his uniqueness, an undecidable uniqueness that images the undecidability of the Other, the memory of that which makes possible his hope for the possible just community. Moses replaced faithful memory and hope, enacted in covenant, with certainty and control. By deciding his origin, he replaced his uniqueness with his mere individuality and left the community.

Contrary to what the diagram of Moses' life might suggest by itself, his life is no more completed in history than is the community. For the end of the chiasmus drawn for Moses is not community, but the birth of community. We see Moses begin the labor of community. That labor is the end of Moses' life. As ἔσχατον, that end gives Moses' life its shape, so we have no need to see his life's last moment—especially since the origin of community (whether beginning or end) is outside the limit of any individual's or community's life.

This gives us something to say in response to our question of Kant— namely, how is it possible to take into account otherness and, therefore, to be charitable? Neither modernism—in other words, secularism—nor much that calls itself postmodernism can deal with that difficulty. Both drive us either to historicism, with no interruption of history, or to nihilism, with nothing but interruption. The story of Moses and Israel shows the difference between secular and hypersecular, on the one hand, and religious community, on the other. Modernism's confidence denies the covenantal character of the labor for justice by taking the origin of community either as a determinate beginning (as in nationalism and racism), as a determinate apocalypse (as in Stalinism), or as completely indeterminate (as in nihilism). Our answer to Kant is that the origin is both determinate and indeterminate. Charity is possible because there is a determinate origin disrupted by indeterminacy.

Like the biblical community, a community that I describe as postsecular,[13] much postmodernism sees the impossibility of the labor for justice. The difference between the impossibility that characterizes postsecular community and the impossibility of postmodern community is what seems almost an indifference. Though both recognize the impossibility of justice, the postsecular do so with an eye toward the justice that remains yet to come, for those who remain "over there." They labor for the apocalypse and for salvic history and, therefore, in hope. Unlike the modern or the postmodern, the postsecular refuse to decide the determinacy/indeterminacy of origin. They leave that origin undecided within the historical particularity of their community's beginning and apocalypse.

Neither the postsecular nor the hypermodern can see beyond beginning and end, the ἔσχατον, the shape or outline, of community. Neither can see its origin except as that origin shows itself historically and contextually. Thus, the hypermodern see what seems to be the same impossibility that the postsecular see. They see it, however, without hope. For the hypermodern thinker, courage or resignation in the face of this impossibility must be enough. Having decided that the origin is merely indeterminate, nothing other than history and no trace of any determinate other justifies the hope for justice. However, by remembering and anticipating the origin—in other words, by being attentive to the trace of origin in its attention to beginning and apocalypse—the biblical community goes beyond courage to memory, covenant, and hope. Odd as it may seem, a hopeful postsecular community, rather than the brave hypermodern community, would refuse to decide the origin, for to see the origin as beginning or apocalypse without hope or not to see it at all, not even as a trace, is to have decided it to be nothing. On the other hand, to see the impossibility of justice hopefully is *not* to decide it; it is to see its necessity as well as its impossibility.

Because both the hypermodern and the modern assume that the origin of community is determinate, for them final justice must be universal—if there is justice at all. For them, to the degree that justice is particular, it fails as justice. They do not see that merely universal justice would be absolutely *un*just, for it would demand that we ignore the particularities of the individuals with whom we deal and, therefore, that we treat them unjustly. To ignore the embodied differences between us by recourse to universals is to spiritualize human being. It is a murderous attack on persons because it severs their spirits from their bodies, as if one could exist without the other. Only a refusal to decide the origin can prevent such murder. But a guarantee that murder will not happen is impossible. Apostasy and murder necessarily haunt the shadows of the community; they are the underside of the labor for justice and its transcendent impossibility.

No argument or phenomenology will show the possibility of going beyond hypermodern courage or resignation to postsecular hope. There are at least two reasons for this. First, the chiasmus of Moses' life showed us the birth of the community in tension and death. Murder always threatens to take the place of the search for justice. The incomplete chiasmus of Israel's history shows that the dissolution of community is an always immanent possibility. The just community always stands on the verge of dissolution, of apostasy. To labor for something is for that thing to remain as yet unrealized. To labor is to be underway, but not yet "there," and, so, to be necessarily in danger of not arriving. Thus, without the risk of murder and apostasy, no labor for justice would be possible. The violence at each major point in the chiasmus and the contrast between that violence and the disruption of the epiphany suggest the omnipresence of this risk.

Second, these chiasmi are structured around the epiphany, the disruption of history by God's name. The vertical epiphany disrupts the horizontal plane of both the individual and the community and their history. Strictly speaking, however, such a disruption is unnecessary. It is gratuitous; it appears, if at all, as only a trace. We are within the horizontal plane of history and can give no certain evidence for a transcendent disruption.[14] The demand for certain evidence occurs outside of the context in which the transcendent disruption can be understood, for it asks for determination of that which must remain, in an important sense, indeterminate. The enactment of origin in the labor for justice occurs within a community defined by the epiphany of transcendence, but there is no evidence for the transcendent more than the community enacted by it.

For the postsecular community, the problem is where to find this transcendent disruption; traditionally and still for many, it is found in religious communities. Is postsecular, but nonreligious, community possible? If not, then outside the religious community, the labor for the just community is, at best, an undecidable alternation between hope and terror. Perhaps only terror, for nothing authorizes hope.

Whether community is possible, except in God's name, remains a question, a question attached to a hope. Nevertheless, the story of Moses and Israel suggests at least this much: Without some Name, the vertical disruption of history is impossible or meaningless: tyranny is unavoidable. Without a Name, there is no difference between a founding disruption and the violence at the boundaries of the horizontal: those it ignores or kills define the community. Without a Name, we think the beginning as only *our* beginning: nationalism, racism, and destiny. Without a Name, we can think the apocalypse only negatively, as the end of history, the destruction of everything, the dissolution of the labor for justice: the Red Guard and the Cultural Revolution. Without a Name, those who stand at the margins of history and community are subjects and objects of violence and can have no other relation to us: justice is a matter of only reciprocity, something reserved for our alter egos. Without a Name, the community cannot be a community of hope.

The question is whether there can be another Name than God's. That remains to be seen. For philosophy, however, the question is not what other names there might be, but whether philosophy can utter *any* Name. Philosophy cannot give content to the rupture of transcendence, for it cannot name what remains outside. But can it say something else, something that avoids such naming? Or can it, like biblical religion, utter a name that continues to be indeterminate and interruptive even in its determination?

The biblical story of Moses and Israel suggests that justice is possible because transcendence is both rupture and call—both the call of one's heritage and the call of those who stand at the margins of one's future, questioning—rather than merely determinate content.[15] Rupture and call always occur within a content. They require a determinate content or they are not rupture and call. But they are neither rupture nor call *because of* that content. Rupture and call are what they are in virtue of what remains unsaid and unsayable in them. Biblical religion suggests that we look for transcendence not by looking beyond this world, but by looking within this world for that which calls us to justice by breaking or interrupting our understanding of justice. Though imagination and the Golden Rule cannot make justice possible because they can give us only reciprocity and not transcendence, biblical religion suggests that the principle of charity, and so justice, is possible because interruption is possible. The Bible teaches us to look for justice by remembering that we are constituted by a disrupted origin and called toward an ever-receding purity of justice: for biblical religion, transcendence is to be found in immanence and in the rupture of immanence by that which calls from beyond the margins of our communities.

NOTES

1. It is more accurate to say that my religious belief is the field in which my other beliefs make sense than it is to say that my religious belief is one set of beliefs among others (see my "Scripture as Incarnation"), but that is not crucial to this paper.

2. Gadamer makes a similar point in *Truth and Method* (e.g., 202–203 and 354–360).

3. For an example of some current work on this issue, see Simon.

4. See Ricoeur 140–150 [115–124]. (Numbers in brackets in the citations refer to the translation.)

5. See my "Uncanny Interruption."

6. Henry's example is instructive: we often assume that the notion of transcendence that we find in the New Testament is a notion of otherworldly transcendence when, in fact, it is a notion of embodied transcendence, transcendence in this world (see 11–19). Whether Henry's claim to have offered a new kind of phenomenology is justified is irrelevant to my point. I am not arguing for that claim, a claim about which I have doubts. My point is only that Henry is right to point out that first-century and later Christianity was a scandal to those who believed in otherworldly transcendence precisely because of its emphasis on the body and this world. As a result, it is a mistake to assume that biblical religion, and particularly Christianity, thinks transcendence as merely otherworldly.

7. I am grateful to the Institute of Philosophy, Catholic University of Leuven, for the time as a visiting professor during which I wrote much of the analysis of Moses and

Israel in 1995–96. I am especially grateful to Professor Paul Moyaert for his encouragement and Professor Rudi Visker for his criticisms. I also appreciate the support of Brigham Young University for my leaves of absence.

8. The literature on the meaning of this name is voluminous, but explicating the various ways of interpreting it is not central to this paper, so I pass over them roughshod.

9. See Deuteronomy 10:17–19: "For the Lord your God . . . regardeth not persons, nor taketh reward: He doth execute the judgment of the fatherless and widow, and loveth the stranger, in giving him food and raiment. Love ye therefore the stranger: *for ye were strangers in the land of Egypt*" (my emphasis).

10. Though there is not enough room here to make the point textually, the story of Man and Woman in the Garden shows that the origin is also irrecuperable as beginning.

11. The Christian interpretation of Judaism often recognizes that there can be no law without what transcends the Law. Less often, however, do Christians recognize that the transcendent without the Law is meaningless.

12. It is not clear where Moses' failure was, in taking credit for the water or in striking the rock to bring forth water rather than speaking to it as God had commanded him. In either case, the point remains the same.

13. I borrow this term from Martin.

14. I am sympathetic to Marion's arguments for the phenomenological character of this disruption. (See his essay in this volume and the essay "The Saturated Phenomenon.") However, as both Han and Zarader point out (also in this volume) that part of his argument which is least disputable is the part that is most like Heidegger's. See also Janicaud's discussion of Marion (39–56 [50–69]) and Ricoeur's criticism of Levinas (387–393 [335–341]), a criticism that also applies to Marion. Thus, the reference to a vertical disruption should be understood as an interpretive reference within the biblical story. It is not an attempt to claim, implicitly, that the disruption must be the disruption of a Higher Being.

15. There are many places to read about this biblical theme, particularly about the ontological importance of the call. However, though not the center of Zarader's focus, her book *La dette impensée* contains an excellent, recent discussion of the issue (57–69).

WORKS CITED

Faulconer, James E. "Scripture as Incarnation." In Paul Y. Hoskisson, ed., *Historicity and the Latter-day Saints Scriptures*, 17–61. Provo, Utah: Religious Studies Center, Brigham Young University, 2001.

———. "The Uncanny Interruption of Ethics: Gift, Interruption, or . . ." *The Graduate Faculty Philosophy Journal* 20–21, No. 1–2 (1998): 233–247.

Gadamer, Hans-Georg. *Truth and Method.* 2nd rev. ed. Trans. Joel Weinsheimer and Donald G. Marshall. New York: Continuum, 1993.

Henry, Michel. *Incarnation. Une philosophie de la chair.* Paris: Seuil, 2000.

Janicaud, Dominique. *Le tournant théologique de la phénoménologie française.* Paris: L'Éclat, 1991. Translated as *The Theological Turn in French Phenomenology.* Trans. Bernard G. Prusack. In Dominique Janicaud, Jean-François Courtine, Jean-Louis Chrétien, Michel Henry, Jean-Luc Marion, and Paul Ricoeur, *Phenomenology and the "Theological Turn": The French Debate*, 16–103. New York: Fordham University Press, 2000.

Levinas, Emmanuel. *Totalité et infini, Essai sur l'extériorité*. The Hague: Martinus Nijhoff, 1961. Translated as *Totality and Infinity: An Essay on Exteriority*. Trans. Alphonso Lingis. Pittsburgh: Duquesne University Press, 1969.

Martin, Bill. *Matrix and Line: Derrida and the Possibilities of Postmodern Social Theory*. Albany: SUNY Press, 1992.

Nachmanides. *Commentary on the Torah: Exodus*. Trans. Charles B. Chavel. New York: Shilo Publishing House, 1973.

Ricoeur, Paul. *Soi-même comme un autre*. Paris: Seuil, 1990. Translated as *Oneself as Another*. Trans. Kathleen Blamey. Chicago: University of Chicago Press, 1992.

Simon, Josef. "Philosophie critique et Écriture sainte." *Revue de Métaphysique et de Morale* 4 (October–December 2000): 441–460.

Zarader, Marlène. *La dette impensée. Heidegger et l'héritage hébraïque*. Paris: Seuil, 1990.

PART II. RETHINKING PHENOMENOLOGY FROM RELIGION

The Event, the Phenomenon, and the Revealed

Jean-Luc Marion

I. What Shows Itself and What Gives Itself

Every phenomenon appears, but it appears only to the extent that it shows itself. Heidegger convincingly demonstrated that the phenomenon is defined as what shows itself in itself and from itself. Still, he left the question of how to think the *self* at work in what shows *itself* largely undetermined.[1] How in fact can a phenomenon claim to deploy itself, if a transcendental *I* constitutes it as an object placed at the disposition of and by the thought that fully penetrates it?

In such a world—the world of technical objects, our world for the most part—phenomena can only reach the rank of objects. Thus their phenomenality is merely borrowed, and it is as if they are derived from the intentionality and the intuition that we grant to them. To admit the contrary, that a phenomenon shows itself, one would have to be able to acknowledge it to be a *self* that initiates its manifestation. The question is, then, to know whether and how such an initiation of manifestation can befall a phenomenon. I have proposed the following response: a phenomenon can show *itself* only to the extent that it gives *itself* first—nothing can show *itself* unless it gives *itself* first. Still, as we will see, the reverse is not necessarily true, since what gives *itself* need not show *itself*—the given² is not always phenomenalized. How, then, to get a bearing on what gives itself? The givenness of self cannot be seen directly, since what can be seen must have shown itself already—or at least, in the case of objects, it must have been shown. If manifestation perhaps proceeds from the given, then the given has to precede it; the given is therefore anterior to manifestation. In other words, the given is not yet implicated in the space of visibility and so, strictly speaking, is unseen. Therefore, we could not access the given, the movement through which the phenomenon gives *itself*, by outlining the visibility of what possibly shows itself there—assuming, of course, that a non-objective phenomenality could manifest itself that way. Only one solution remains: to try to locate, in the very space of manifestation, the regions where phenomena show *themselves*, instead of simply letting themselves be shown as objects. Or, to isolate regions where the *self* of what shows *itself* testifies indisputably to the thrust, the pressure, and, so to speak, the impact of what gives *itself*. The *self* of what shows *itself* would then manifest indirectly that it gives *itself* in a more fundamental sense. This same *self*, located in the phenomenon showing *itself*, would come from the original *self* of that which gives itself. Better: the *self* of phenomenalization would then manifest indirectly the *self* of the given, because the one would employ the other and ultimately coincide with it.

Yet, how can we detect such an ascension from the phenomenalizing *self* to the giving *self*? Which phenomena retain the trace of their donation in them, to the point that their mode of phenomenalization not only gives access to their originary *self*, but also renders it incontestable? Consider the following hypothesis: the phenomena in question have the character of an event. In fact, though the event seems to be a phenomenon like any other, it can be distinguished from objective phenomena in that it is not a result of a process of production. The event is not a product, determined and foreseen, predictable on the basis of its causes, and reproducible through the repetition of these causes. On the contrary, in happening the event testifies to an unpredictable origin, arising due to largely unknown or even absent causes, causes that are at least unassignable, such that one does not know how to reproduce it, for its constitution has no sense. Still, it could be objected that such events are rare, that their very unpredictability renders them unsuitable for analyzing manifestation—in short, that they provide no solid ground for an inquiry into the given. Can this seemingly obvious objection be challenged? I shall try to do so, choosing a most trivial example: this room, the *Salle des Actes* of the Catholic Institute, where today's academic meeting is being held.

Even this auditorium appears in the mode of an event. Do not protest that it lets itself be seen in the manner of an object—four walls, a false ceiling hiding a balcony, a podium, a certain number of seats, all available in the manner of permanent and subsistent beings that exist, waiting for us to inhabit them and use them or for us to certify their subsistence. For, curiously, this permanence in waiting signifies the opposite of objective availability.

a. According to the Past

As always already there, available for our arrival and usage, this hall imposes itself on us as preceding us, being without us even if for us. It appears to our view as an unexpected, unpredictable fact, originating in an uncontrollable past. The surprise of this unexpected appearance does not apply only to the rooms of this particular Romanesque palace, often passed by in the walks about town of an ignorant tourist or in the hurried march of a blasé inhabitant of the Eternal City, but which sometimes, in response to an exceptional invitation, on entering we suddenly discover in all its unpredictable and, until now, unknown splendor. The surprise applies equally well to the *Salle des Actes*—already there, emerging from a past of which we are unaware. Redecorated many times thanks to now forgotten restoration projects, weighed down with a history exceeding our memory (could it be a converted cloister?), it forces itself upon me when it appears. It is not so much that I enter this room as that the room itself comes to me, engulfs me, and imposes itself upon me. This "already" testifies to the event.

b. According to the Present

Here, the nature of the event of the phenomenon of this hall shines forth. For it is no longer a question of the *Salle des Actes* as such, in general, subsisting as an indifferent vacuity between this or that occasion that fills it with an undifferentiated public. It is a question of this *Salle* this evening, filled for this occasion, to hear these speakers on this topic. This evening, the *Salle des Actes* becomes a hall—in the theatrical sense of a good or bad hall. It becomes a stage—in the theatrical sense that this or that actor can first fill it, then keep the attention of the audience. Finally, it is a question of a hall, where what comes to pass is neither the walls nor the stones, neither the spectators nor the speakers, but the intangible event that their words will take hold of, making it understood or spoiling it. This moment will certainly be inserted among other academic meetings, other conferences, other university ceremonies, but it will never be repeated as such. This evening, devoted to this topic and not any other, among us and no others, an absolutely unique, irreproducible, and largely unpredictable event, is being played out—after all, at the precise moment that I say "the precise moment," neither you, nor the presiding dean, nor I, none of us knows yet whether it will turn out to be a success or a failure. What appears at this precise moment under our eyes escapes all constitution: having been organized with clear, friendly, intellectual, and social intentions, it shows *itself* of itself from itself nevertheless. The *self* of that which gives *itself* announces itself in this "*self*" of its phenomenality. The "this time, once and for all" testifies then also to the *self* of the phenomenon.

c. In the Future

Even after the event, no witness, however knowledgeable, attentive, and backed up by documents as he or she might be, can describe what is happening at the moment. The event of this public oral presentation, made possible by a consenting audience and a benevolent institution, engages not only material means—itself impossible to describe exhaustively, stone by stone, epoch by epoch, attendee by attendee—but also an undefined intellectual framework. After all, I must explain what I say and what I mean to say, from where I say it, with what presuppositions I begin, from what texts, from what personal and spiritual problems. It would also be necessary to describe the motivations of each listener: their expectations; their disappointments; their agreements, masked in silence or exaggerated by polemic. Then, in order to describe what kind of event has happened in this "hall," this *Salle des Actes*, it would be necessary to follow the consequences for the individual and collective evolution of all the participants, the main speaker included—which, fortunately, is impossible. Such a hermeneutics would deploy itself without end and in no defined network.[3] No exhaustive and reproducible constitution of an object can be at work here. The "without end" shows that the event arose from itself, that its phenomenality arose from the *self* of its givenness.

This opening analysis, precisely because it is based on a phenomenon that is, at first sight, simple and banal, assures us that showing-*itself* can give indirect access to the *self* of that which gives *itself*. The event of this "hall," the *Salle des Actes*, makes a phenomenon appear before us that not only neither arises out of our initiative, nor responds to our expectations, nor can ever be reproduced, but which above all gives *itself* to us from its own *self*, to the point that it affects us, changes us, almost produces us. We can never stage an event (nothing would be more ridiculously contradictory than the supposed "organization of the event"); rather, it stages us[4] out of the initiative of its own *self* by *giving itself to us*. It stages us in the scene opened by its givenness.

II. The Event as the Self of the Given Phenomenon

This analysis, however rigorous it may be, encounters a difficulty, or at least something strange: it considers as an event what at first sight is an object—in this case, the hall. On what basis can an object be interpreted as an event—a hall as a "hall"? If we follow that line of thinking, in the end could not every object be described as an event? Should not a more reasonable distinction be maintained between these two concepts? And what is gained from such an interpretation? After all, the object certainly belongs to the sphere of phenomenality, yet it is not evident that the phenomenon still comes under it.

To answer these sensible objections, one must undoubtedly turn the question around and ask, on the contrary, how can the essential and original event character of phenomena (even of the most banal type, like the one that I have just described) grow blurred, attenuate, and disappear, to the point that it appears as no more than an object? One should not ask, Up to what point can one legitimately think the phenomenon as an event? Instead, the question is, Why can one miss phenomenality by reducing it to objectivity?

To reply to this question, we can find inspiration in Kant. The first of the four headings that organize the categories of understanding, and so impose onto phenomena the quadruple seal of objectivity, refers to quantity. Kant points out that to become an object, every phenomenon must possess a quantity, a magnitude. Given this magnitude, the totality of the phenomenon equals and results from the sum total of its parts. From this follows another decisive feature: it can and must be possible to anticipate the object on the basis of the sum of the parts that compose it, such that it is always "intuited in advance [*schon angeschaut*[5]] as an aggregate (the sum of parts given in advance [*vorher angeschaut*])" (A163; B204). That certainly signifies that the magnitude of the phenomenon can, by right, always be modeled in a finite quantity, and so be inscribed in a real space or be transcribed (by means of models, parameters, and encoding) into an imaginary space. It signifies above all that the phenomenon is inscribed in a space that we can always know in advance by summing its parts. This hall has a quantity that results from the sum of its parts—these walls delimit its volume and also indicate other nonextended parameters (its fabrication and maintenance cost, occupancy rate, etc.) that specify budgetary costs and its pedagogical use. In principle, no place is left in it for the least surprise: what appears will always inscribe itself in what the sum of these parameters already permits us to foresee. The hall is foreseen before it is actually seen—confined in its quantity, defined through its parts, brought to a halt, so to say, by the measurements that precede it and await its empirical execution (its construction). This reduction of the hall to its foreseeable quantity turns it into an object, before and in which we pass as if there were nothing else to be seen in it, nothing other than what can already be envisaged on the basis of its construction plan. The same applies to all technical objects: we no longer see them—we no longer need to see them, since we foresee them far in advance. And we succeed in using them all the better if we can foresee them without being preoccupied with seeing them. We only need to begin to see them when we can no longer or do not yet foresee them—that is, when we can no longer or do not yet use them (in other words, when they break down or when we are learning to use them). Within the limits of typical technical usage, we thus have no need to see objects; it suffices for us to foresee them. We thus reduce them to the rank of second order, common law, phenomena, deprived of full—that is, autonomous and disinterested—appearance. They appear transparent to us, in the neutral light of objectivity. Of what is a phenomenon foreseen and not seen, turned into an object, deprived? When we style it a foreseen phenomenon, is it not this very foresight that disqualifies it as a full phenomenon? What does foresight mean here? That in the object everything remains seen in advance, that nothing unexpected will turn up—costs, occupancy, utility, and so on. The object remains a phenomenon that has expired because it appears as something that has always already expired: nothing new can happen to it, since, more radically, under the regard that constitutes it, it appears as what cannot happen at all. The object appears as the shadow of the event that we deny in it.

Still, we could invert the analysis and move from the object, the transparent phenomenon deprived of any ability to happen, to its original phenomenality, governed part and parcel by eventiality [*l'événementialité*]—following the rule of essence that what truly shows *itself* must first give *itself*. We have in fact already accomplished this move from the object to the event by describing the common-law phenomenon—this "hall" that is precisely not the *Salle des Actes*—as a triple event, according to the "already" of its facticity, the "this time, once and for all" of its realization, and the "without end" of its hermeneutics. It remains, then, to return to the description of the evential character of phenomenality in general, referring from now on to phenomena that can unquestionably be thematized as events. First, collective phenomena are called by the title of event ("historical": political revolution, war, natural disaster, cultural or sport event, etc.), and they satisfy at least three requirements.

> a. They cannot be repeated identically, and thus they show themselves to be identical only to themselves: irreproducibility, hence irreversibility.
>
> b. They can be assigned neither a unique cause nor an exhaustive explanation; the number of causes and possible explanations is indefinite and increases in proportion to the hermeneutic that historians, sociologists, economists, and others can develop to their purposes—exceeding the number of effects and facts of any system of causes.
>
> c. They cannot be foreseen, since their partial causes not only remain insufficient, but are discovered only after the effect has been accomplished. It follows that their possibility, impossible to foresee, remains, strictly speaking, an impossibility with regard to the system of previously classified causes. Importantly, these three requirements do not refer exclusively to collective phenomena; they also define private or intersubjective phenomena.

Let us analyze an exemplary and yet banal case, that of Montaigne's friendship for *La Boétie*. The canonical determinants of a phenomenon as an event, which I have developed elsewhere, can be found in it.[6] Friendship with another forces me, first of all, to have regard toward him, a regard that does not follow my intentionality toward him, but submits itself to the point of view that he has toward me, thus placing me at the exact point where his own intention awaits to expose me. This anamorphosis is described precisely by Montaigne: "We looked for each other before we saw one another." To look for each other means that, like rivals who provoke and eye each other up and down, each tried to place himself where the look of the other could come to rest on him. In other words, "It is the I-don't-know-what quintessence of this union that, having seized my will, made it plunge and lose itself in his." I take for myself his point of view on me, without reducing it to my point of view on him; and thus it happens to me. Second, the event of this friendship happens all at once, unforeseen and without warning, in the shape of an unexpected and syncopated *arrival*: "At our first meeting, we found ourselves so absorbed, so familiar, so committed one to the other, that nothing appeared to us so close as the other." Thus it is an always "already" accomplished fact that its *facticity*, "by chance during a great feast and city festival," renders it irreversible rather than weakening it. Third, the phenomenon that gives itself gives nothing other than itself; its ultimate meaning remains inaccessible because it is reduced to the accomplished fact, to its *incidence*. This accident does not indicate any substance; if it signifies more than itself, the surplus remains as unknowable as the "order from heaven" that alone inspires it. From this follows the last feature that characterizes most perfectly the eventiality of the phenomenon: we can assign it neither cause nor reason; or, rather, no reason or cause other than itself, in the pure energy of its unquestionable happening: "If pushed to say why I loved him, I feel that nothing could express this but saying, because it was him, because it was me" (Montaigne 139). The phenomenon of friendship thus shows itself only insofar as, as a pure and perfect event, its phenomenality forces itself upon the mode of being of the event so that it gives itself without question or reserve.

In this way, the eventiality governing every phenomenon, even the most objective in appearance, demonstrates without exception that what shows *itself* can do so only in virtue of a strictly and eidetically phenomenological *self*, which guarantees only that it gives *itself* and that, in return, it proves that its phenomenalization presupposes its givenness as such and from itself.

III. The Time of the Self

Consider the result: the *self* of what shows itself—that is, the phenomenon—testifies, by its universal and intrinsic evential character, that it gives itself originarily. Does that not lead to a banal conclusion that every phenomenon, even the intuitively poor or common-law object, is temporal? In that case, would we not simply return to a position that is, quite classically, Kantian? Undoubtedly—if we were to accept two inadmissible corollaries of Kant's critique.

First, this one: temporality serves only to permit the synthesis of phenomena as objects, thus working to assure permanence in presence. Now, my analysis establishes exactly the contrary: temporality originarily brings about the happening of occurrences as accomplished fact, with neither reason nor cause and by imposing an anamorphosis. In short, it allows phenomenality to be understood under the mode of event, contrary to all objectivity, which becomes at best a residual case, provisionally permanent, illusorily subsistent.

Temporality does not work for the sake of objects, but in favor of the event, which undoes and overdetermines the object, which, to repeat, is simply the illusion of an atemporal event.

The other corollary: temporality as internal sense belongs to sensibility and operates only by orienting the subject toward the synthesis of known objects; still, the transcendental *I*, the operator of this synthesis (of syntheses), even though it puts temporality to work in a masterly manner, is not itself defined *strictly as such* according to this temporality. Even if we suppose that phenomena temporalized as objects preserve a trace of eventiality (which is open to question), still the transcendental *I* itself, however temporalizing it might be, absolutely does not phenomenalize itself as an event. And it does not for a reason that is absolutely determinative: it never phenomenalizes itself, does not appear amongst other phenomena, as it is excluded from the phenomenality that it produces. Having said this, we cannot overcome the Kantian objection with only negative arguments. To truly overcome it, it will be necessary to identify phenomena temporalized eidetically as events; temporalized in such a way that they provoke the ego to phenomenalize itself according to this unique eventiality. Can we adduce such a phenomenon?

A premier case of such a phenomenon presents itself: death, a phenomenon that can be phenomenalized only in *its* coming to pass, for outside of this passage it cannot properly be; it appears, then, only to the extent that it comes to pass; if it didn't, it could never be. Death can only show *itself* by giving itself as an event. It could never let itself be seen otherwise. Still, when it happens, what does it show of itself? Is it not subject to the classical aporia according to which, as long as I am, death is not, and when it happens, I am no longer there to see it? Does it not provide only the illusion of an event, the illusion that a phenomenon gives *itself*? To reply, we must provide a somewhat more precise description and distinguish between the death of the other and my own death.

The death of the other appears to the extent that *it* comes to pass, but it consists precisely in the pure and simple passage, itself not real, from the state of a living being to that of a corpse. This passage cannot be seen directly. Unlike the two states it traverses, as a phenomenon the death of the other lasts only the instant of the passage (even if the funeral ceremony tries to make it last and does so for the very reason that the passage lasted only a moment). The death of the other shows *itself* only in a flash and it gives *itself* only in withdrawing—by removing the living other from us. It is a pure phenomenon, to be sure, yet too pure to show *itself* and so give *itself* as a perfect event. And this is even more true since this flash of event does not involve my ego, since, by enclosing me in my residual life, the death of the other bars all access to both the other and to death.

My own death involves me completely, to be sure, and it also appears only in coming to pass, and thus as an event testifying to a phenomenal givenness. However, an obvious aporia compromises its relevance: if death comes to pass upon me (supposing that a phenomenon manifests itself in this passage), insofar as I pass away together with it, I could never see the event. Certainly, this aporia poses a threat only from the point of view of one who has not yet experienced this passage, who does not know whether it will annihilate or "change" me (1 Corinthians 15:52). Thus, this aporia of my death only matters to one who, like all us of here, has not yet died. We are ignorant as to whether that which gives death is an event or a nihilation of phenomenality. In fact, the human condition is primarily characterized neither by death (animals and civilizations die as well) nor by the consciousness of ending in death, but by the ignorance of what happens (or shows *itself*) to me at the moment when death comes upon me. My death does not, then, place me before an effectivity or a passage. Rather, it places me before a simple possibility—the possibility of impossibility. And this possibility of impossibility, which will necessarily give *itself*, retains until the end the possibility of not showing *itself*, of not showing anything. Hence the event of my death, the closest, the least far away, from which only one heartbeat separates me, remains inaccessible to me by the excess in it (and it is, provisionally at least, inevitable), by the excess of its pure donation to phenomenality. There, too, we are surely dealing with a pure phenomenon, but one too pure to show *itself* and so to give *itself* as a perfect event. This phenomenon, which deserves the title of an event and which involves me in it radically because it gives *itself*, nevertheless withdraws as a phenomenon that shows *itself*.

How can we proceed? Let us return to the phenomenon itself: it gives *itself* in that it shows *itself*, yet only insofar as the manifestation occurs in it in the mode of a happening that falls before my gaze as an accomplished fact (an incident) that it appropriates (anamorphosis). Obviously, these determinations refer to time, which the event radically presupposes. Yet does the event not involve time as one of its elements or conditions? Certainly not. For time itself first happens in the mode of an event. Husserl saw that and defined time as starting from an "original impression" that, as a "source point," continuously arises in and as the pure present, and that, precisely because it occurs, does not cease to pass into the no-longer-present, a time retained by retention before sinking into the past (*Internal Time* §11). The present arises as first and the first comes to pass as pure event—unpredictable, irreversible, irreproducible as such, immediately past and deprived of cause or reason. It alone escapes objectivity, even though it makes it possible, because it is absolutely excluded from all constitution: "The originary impression is a non-modifiable absolute, the original source for all consciousness and being to come" (§31). Here the movement of that which gives *itself* is accomplished and almost no possibility of appearing is left to that which shows *itself*, since the originary impression changes immediately and, as soon as it arises, lives continually in retention. Still, unlike death, this excess of givenness does not prevent an event from being effectively and even sensibly accomplished, since the originary impression does not cease to reappear from the absolute unseen, from the shadow out of which it emerges. The originary impression gives *itself* to *be seen* as a pure event relentlessly brought to life through indefinite and unconditional birth. From the "source point," givenness unremittingly at work, what hardly shows *itself* (this instant) is born from each instant of that which gives *itself* completely (the originary impression).

Birth—here we have a phenomenon that shows *itself* truly in the mode of what gives *itself*, the phenomenon that is properly evential. The question is how to understand my birth showing *itself* as a phenomenon, since, properly speaking, I have never actually seen it with my own eyes and, in order to reconstitute it, I must rely on eye witnesses or administrative decisions. Though it takes place without me and even, strictly speaking, before me, it should not be able to show *itself* (if it showed itself) to anybody other than me. Still, I consider it a phenomenon, since I continuously intend it (I want to know who I am and where I come from, I search for personal identity, etc.) and I fulfill these intentions with quasi-intuitions (second-hand memories, direct and indirect testimony, etc.). My birth appears even as a privileged phenomenon, since a significant part of my life is devoted to reconstituting it, giving it sense, and responding to its silent call. Still, in principle I cannot see this unquestionable phenomenon directly. This aporia could be formalized by saying that my birth shows me precisely that my origin cannot be shown—in short, that it attests only to the originary non-originality of the origin [*l'originaire non-originelleité de l'origine*].[7] This must be understood in a double sense. Either my birth happens before I can see and receive it, in which case I am not present at my own origin, or my birth. My origin is in itself nothing originary but flows from an indefinite series of events and appearances (*sumque vel a parentibus productus*) (Descartes 145). However, to describe this aporia is not yet to resolve it. It remains to be understood how a phenomenon that does not show *itself* (and in a sense it does show itself well through numerous intermediaries) not only affects me as if it did show itself, but also affects me more radically than any other, since it alone determines me, defines my ego, even produces it. Put otherwise: if an origin cannot in general show *itself*, all the less can an origin be dispossessed of its originarity. How then does this originary non-originality happen to me—since it happens to me, has happened to me, I come to it—if it remains necessarily indemonstrable? It happens to me exactly in that it happens, and happens [*advenir*] only in that it endows me with a future [*l'avenir*]. My birth is not called a phenomenon (that of the non-originary origin) because it shows *itself*, but because, in the very absence of any direct monstration, it comes to pass as an event that was never present and always already dated [*passé*], but never outdated [*dépassé*]—in fact, always to-come. My birth does phenomenalize *itself*, but as a pure event, unpredictable, irreproducible, exceeding all cause, and making the impossible possible (that is to say, my always new life), surpassing all expectation, all promise, and all prediction. This phenomenon, which is accomplished in a perfect reduction of that which shows *itself*, thus testifies in an exceptional and paradigmatic way that its phenomenality flows directly from the fact that it gives *itself*.

We thus find what we have been looking for: all that shows *itself* not only gives *itself*, but gives *itself* as an event according to a temporality that is itself evential, to the point that, in exceptional cases (birth), a phenomenon directly succeeds in giving *itself* without showing *itself*.

In fact, a number of characteristics justify the phenomenological privilege granted to birth:

a. The phenomenon of birth gives *itself* directly without showing *itself* directly because it comes to pass as an event par excellence (an origin originally non-originary). Nevertheless, this excellence follows from the fact that it *gives me to myself* when it gives *itself*. It phenomenalizes itself by affecting me, but it affects me not only by giving me to myself, but (since without it I would not yet be there to be affected by it) by giving a *myself* a *me*, which receives itself from what it receives.[8]

b. From the beginning, the phenomenon of birth takes to its height the inclusion of the ego in eventiality by founding that ego in an exemplary way as the given-to:[9] the one that receives itself from what it receives. The phenomenon of birth exemplifies the phenomenon in general—something can phenomenalize itself only to the extent that it gives *itself*. However, at the same time, it institutes the given-to (originarily a posteriori since it receives itself from what it receives), the first phenomenon (making possible the reception of all others).

c. Thus, the phenomenon of birth gives *itself* as a full-fledged saturated phenomenon (or paradox). In effect, its event, the first originating impression and so more originary than any other instant, makes possible an indefinite, indescribable, and unpredictable series of originating impressions to come—those that accumulate in the span of my life and that define me until the end of my life. In this way birth opens the course of innumerable temporal intuitions, for which I unceasingly, but always too late, will seek to find significations, concepts, and noeses that will inevitably remain insufficient. I will always try to find the words to tell (myself) what will happen to me, or rather, what will have already happened to me, without being able to adequately explain, understand, or constitute it when it happens. The excess of intuition over intention bursts forth from my birth on—and moreover, I will speak not so much because I have intended silently, but above all after hearing others speak. Language is heard first and spoken only afterwards. The origin certainly remains inaccessible not because of its deficiency, but because the first phenomenon already saturates every intention with intuitions. The origin, which refuses to show itself, does not, however, give *itself* through poverty (Derrida), but through excess, thus determining the organization of all the givens to come. That is to say, that nothing shows *itself* unless it first gives *itself*.

IV. Is the Reduction to the Given Self-Contradictory?

Let us take it as granted that the phenomenon, considered in its radical evential character, reduces to the given. Such a given, especially if it is thought in terms of my birth, insofar as it can give *itself* as a spectacle of which I would be a spectator (whether disinterested or not does not matter here) without showing *itself* directly, is accomplished as a saturated phenomenon. It is a saturated phenomenon that, in the event, strikes an ego which, under that blow [*coup*], becomes a given-to. In effect, such an event gives *itself* at a stroke [*coup*]: it leaves one speechless; it leaves one with no way to escape it; in the end, it leaves one without the choice either to refuse or to voluntarily accept it. Its accomplished fact cannot be discussed, or avoided, or decided. It is not even a question of a kind of violence, since violence implies something arbitrary and, so, an arbiter and an already given space of freedom. It is a question of pure phenomenological necessity: since the event always already gives *itself*, its givenness already bygone and necessarily contingent, as in the case of the birth phenomenon or originary impression, it makes manifest the *self* of that which gives *itself*. It testifies that this phenomenon and, by derivation, all other phenomena can give *themselves* in the strict sense, for it proves that, as a pure event, it makes such a *self* available. Not only does the event give *itself* in itself (canceling the retreat of the thing in itself), but it gives itself from itself and so as a *self*.

The stakes at risk in this analysis should not be underestimated: if the *self* belongs to the phenomenon, no ego can continue to pretend to claim, in first place and first instance, ipseity, the *self*. Does not the ego of Descartes attain its *self* in reply to the *nescio quis* that pertains to it, whether as the deceiver or, rather, as the almighty? Does not *Dasein* arrive at its ipseity by an anticipatory resolution that makes possible the event of nothingness, which it tears out from the ontic? I contend that the attempts, however grandiose they might be, to assign the status of the first self to the ego—in other words, to give the ego transcendental dignity—manage to do no more than to underline the radical primacy of the self of an event, whatever it is (whether an entity in the world, an entity out of the world, or the totality of entities [*l'étant en totalité*]) and whatever it is not. If only for the sake of being concerned, one has to recognize that if the phenomenon truly gives *itself*, it necessarily confiscates the function and the role of the self in the process, thus conceding to the ego only a secondary and derived *me*. And we explicitly draw this conclusion in challenging the claim of every *I* to a transcendental function or, what is the same, the claim of a possible transcendental *I* as the ultimate foundation of the experience of phenomena. Said otherwise: the ego, dispossessed of its transcendental purple,[10] must be admitted as it receives itself, as a given-to: the one who receives itself from what it receives, the one to whom what gives *itself* from a first *self*—every phenomenon—gives a secondary *me*, that of reception and response. Certainly the ego keeps all the privileges of subjectivity, except for the transcendental claim of origin.

The ego is found only in being one to whom is given, endowed with a given *me* and given to receive what gives *itself*. Among the possible objections against such a *diminutio ipseitatis* of the ego, one demands our attention more than the rest because it directly puts into question the phenomenological claim of our enterprise. In fact, for all of phenomenology, the reduction functions, whether explicitly (Husserl) or implicitly (Heidegger, Levinas, Henry, Derrida), as its touchstone; it is nonnegotiable because it is not one concept among others, or a doctrine to be discussed, but an operation that redirects the appearance of appearing to the appearing of phenomena as such. Now, every reduction calls for an agency that operates it—a transcendental *I* or its equivalent (*Dasein*, the face of the other, flesh). Now, the reduction of appearance to the given that we claim to accomplish deviates dangerously from the two other principal reductions that it tries to overcome. First of all, because it does not simply reduce the phenomenon to its constituted object character (Husserl) or to its being-an-entity in being (Heidegger), but ultimately to the given showing *itself* insofar as it gives *itself*—thus establishing the given as an ultimate term and irreducible by any other reduction. And it deviates all the more dangerously because this third reduction leads to the given only by reducing the *I* to the derived and secondary level of the given-to. This reduction of the *I* to the given-to would matter little if it were only a question of a new title and not of another function—the function of receiving oneself from what gives itself and no longer playing the transcendental role, in short, the function of no longer determining the conditions of possibility of experience—in other words, of phenomenality. Now, the reduction, whose task is precisely to change the conditions of the possibility of phenomenality, requires such an a priori *I* (or its transcendental equivalent) and so seems unable to be satisfied with a given-to, something that is by definition a posteriori. In short, the reduction of phenomenon to the givenness of what gives *itself*, going so far as to disqualify the transcendental *I* in a pure and simple given-to, becomes a performative contradiction—it is deprived of the very operator of givenness that it nevertheless claims to make manifest by reduction.

Such a difficulty cannot be resolved all at once. Still, the following needs to be said: if all reductions require an operator that takes us from the appearance of the appearing to the full appearing of the phenomena, then this operator itself is modified in an essential way by the reduction it operates. For Husserl, the phenomenological reduction (not to evoke others that would, no doubt, yield the same result) reduces things of the world to their conscious experience, in view of constituting their intentional objects; still, the *I* reduces itself to its pure immanence ("conscious region"), locating the ensemble of its empirical ego in the transcendence of the "world region" (*Ideas* 140). Thus, the *I* becomes transcendental in the phenomenological sense, since it gets reduced to itself and removed from the natural world by renouncing the natural attitude. For Heidegger, the phenomenological reduction of worldly objects (whether subsistent or common) to their status of beings that are seen according to their diversified ways of being can be brought about only by *Dasein*, the only being in which there is a question of being. Not only is it necessary that *Dasein* accomplish itself as such, and so appropriate its unique way of being and rid itself of the inauthentic mode (that of the "One," which pretends to understand itself as an intra-worldly being); the *Dasein* must then reduce itself to itself—to the status of a being that transcends all other intra-worldly beings in virtue of being itself; this is accomplished during the experience of anxiety. The disappearance of all anthropological determinations (flesh, sexuality, ideology, etc.), with which some have naively reproached *Being and Time*, attests precisely to this modification of "man" into a *Dasein* that turns the reduction onto its agent.

Without trying to compare what cannot be compared, I would say, nevertheless, that the same applies to the third reduction. It is first of all a question of reducing all that claims to appear—object, being, appearance, and so on—to a given. For the formula "as much reduction as givenness" in fact postulates that what the natural attitude accepts with no further ado as a given often is not given yet; or, inversely, that what it finds problematic is in fact absolutely given. It is a question, then, of tracing the necessary connection by which "what shows *itself* must first of all give *itself*" and of giving all the weight to the self, by which only can givenness validate manifestation. Yet how can we imagine that the person, whoever it might be, who makes the reduction to the given and takes "*self*-showing" back to "*self*-giving" by describing the phenomenon as pure event (thus also as anamorphosis, happening, accomplished fact, incident), could leave his own identity uninterrogated, much less keep the identities that correspond so closely to the two preceding reductions? How could he claim to define the conditions of possibility of the experience of phenomena, to which he comes precisely by the third reduction, recognizing that they only show *themselves* in virtue of their *self*, such that he reveals himself in the event in which they give *themselves* and such that he himself establishes the proper conditions of manifestation? If the result of the third reduction, that the phenomenon gives itself from itself, is to be maintained, then the ego can no longer have any transcendental claim. The reduction is not so much compromised, but the reverse. It is realized as in him whom it makes possible, the given-to. The given-to does not compromise the reduction to the given, but confirms it by transferring the *self* from itself to the phenomenon.

This argument sets a second one in motion. The given-to, fallen out of the transcendental rank and the spontaneity or activity that it implies, does not for that turn into passivity or into an empirical me. In fact, the given-to transcends passivity as much as activity, because, liberated from the transcendental purple, it annuls the very distinction between the transcendental *I* and the empirical *me*.

But what third term can there be between activity and passivity, transcendentality and empiricity?

Recall the definition of the given-to: that which *receives* itself from what it receives. The given-to is characterized therefore by reception. To be sure, reception implies passive receptivity, but it also requires active capacity; the capacity (*capacitas*), in order to grow to the measure of the given and to maintain its happening, must put itself to work—the work of the given to be received, the work on itself to receive. The work that the given demands of the given-to, each time and as long as it gives itself, explains why the given-to does not receive once and for all (at birth), but does not cease to receive at the event of each given. Still, this reception can really free the given-to from the dichotomies that incarcerate metaphysical subjectivity only if we understand more clearly its proper phenomenological function. Put otherwise: if the given-to no longer constitutes phenomena, if it is content to receive the pure given and receive itself from it, then what act, what operation, and what role can it still assume in phenomenality itself?

However, in posing this objection to the given-to, we mark an essential gap, that between the given and phenomenality. I repeat what I have often glimpsed before: if all that which shows *itself* must first give itself, then it does not suffice that the given give *itself* in order to show *itself*, since sometimes the givenness almost obscures the manifestation. The given-to has the function precisely of measuring in itself the gap between the given—which never ceases to impose itself upon it and—and phenomenality, which can be realized only to the extent that the reception succeeds in phenomenalizing, or, rather, lets it phenomenalize, itself. This operation, phenomenalizing the given, reverts properly to the given-to in virtue of its difficult privilege of constituting the only given in which the visibility of all other givens happens. The given-to reveals the given as phenomenon.

V. The Revealed

From here on, it is a question of understanding how the given-to reveals (phenomenalizes as an event) the given—and how far it does so.

Let us consider first of all the revealed in a strictly phenomenological sense. First, the given obtained by the reduction: it can be described as that which Husserl called "lived experience," *Erlebnis*. Now—and this crucial point is often forgotten—as such, the lived experience does not show itself, but remains invisible by default. For lack of better words, one can say that it affects me, imposes itself on me, and weighs on what one could dare to call my consciousness (precisely because it does not have yet a clear and distinct consciousness of whatever there is when it receives the pure given). As lived experience, the given remains a *stimulus*, an excitation, hardly information; the given-to receives it, even though it does not show *itself* at all. How does the given sometimes succeed in passing from being unseen to being seen? There is no question here of invoking physiological or psychological considerations, not only due to a lack of knowledge of these subjects, but also in principle: before explaining a process, we must first identify it, and the process wherein the visible arises out of the unseen belongs properly to phenomenology. Following that line of thought, one can take the risk of saying that the given, unseen yet received, projects itself onto the given-to (consciousness, if one prefers) as onto a screen; all the power of that given crashes, as it were, onto this screen, immediately provoking a double visibility.

Certainly, the visibility of the given, the impact of which was invisible until then, explodes and is broken down into outlines, the first visibles. One could also think of the model of the prism, which captures the white light, up to then invisible, and breaks it down into the spectrum of primary colors, rendered light finally visible. The given-to phenomenalizes by receiving the given, precisely because it is an obstacle to the given; it stands in its way, bringing it to a halt in making it a screen and fixing it in a frame. When the given-to receives the given, it receives it with all the vigor, or even the violence, of a goalkeeper defending against the incoming ball, of a defender blocking a return of volley, of a midfielder returning a winning pass. Screen, prism, frame—the given-to collects the impact of the pure unseen given, in retaining the momentum in order to, so to speak, transform its longitudinal force into a spread-out, plane, open surface. With this operation—precisely reception—the given can begin to show *itself*, starting with outlines of visibility that it conceded to the given-to, or, rather, that it received from it.

However, the visibility arising from the given makes the visibility of the given-to arise as well. In fact, the given-to does not see itself before receiving the impact of the given. Deprived of the transcendental purple, the given-to no longer precedes the phenomenon, nor does it any longer "accompany" it as a thought already in place; since it receives itself from what it receives, the given-to does not precede the phenomenon, and certainly not by a visibility that pre-exists the unseen of the given. In fact, the given-to does not show itself more than the given—its screen or prism remains perfectly unseen as long as the impact of a given upon it does not suddenly illuminate it; or, rather, since properly speaking there is no given-to without this reception, the impact gives rise, for the first time, to the screen onto which it crashes, just as it creates the prism across which it is decomposed. In short, the given-to phenomenalizes itself by means of the operation through which it phenomenalizes the given.

Thus, the given reveals itself to the given-to by revealing the given-to to itself. Each phenomenalizes the other as the revealed, which is characterized by this essential phenomenal reciprocity, where seeing implies the modification of the seer by the seen as much as of the seen by the seer. The given-to functions as the revelator of the given and the given as the revelator of the given-to—the revelator being understood here in the photographic sense.[11] Perhaps we could take the risk of saying that the philosophical paradox of quantum physics concerning the interdependence of the object and the observer applies, by analogy, to all of phenomenality without exception. But can we still speak here of "phenomenality without exception"? Have we not previously conceded that, though all that shows *itself* first gives *itself*, the reverse does not apply, since all that gives *itself* does not succeed in showing *itself*? In fact, far from entangling ourselves in a new aporia, we have just found a way out of it. For, if the given shows *itself* only by being blocked and spreading itself on the screen that the given-to has become for it, if the given-to must and can be the only one capable of transforming an impact into visibility, then the extent of phenomenalization depends on the resistance of the given-to to the brute shock of the given. By *resistance* I mean resistance in the sense, suggestive because it is ordinary, of electricity: in a circuit, when one restricts the free movement of electrons—whether by design or accidentally—then a part of their energy is dissipated as heat or light. In this way, the resistance transforms the unseen movement into phenomenalized light and heat. The greater the resistance to the impact of the given (first of all, lived experiences, intuitions), the more that phenomenological light shows *itself*. Resistance—the proper function of the given-to—becomes the index of the transmutation of that which gives itself into that which shows itself. The more the intuitive given increases its pressure, the greater resistance is necessary for the given-to to reveal a phenomenon. From this follows the inevitable and logical hypothesis of saturated phenomena—so saturated with given intuitions that no place is left for corresponding significations and noeses. Faced with such partially nonvisible phenomena (except in the mode of bedazzlement), only the resistance of the given-to can transmute, up to a certain point, the excess of givenness into a fitting monstration—namely, an immeasurable one.

This opens a place for a phenomenological theory of art: the painter makes visible as a phenomenon what no one has ever seen, because, in each case he is the first to succeed in resisting the given enough to make it show *itself*—and then in a phenomenon accessible to all. A great painter never invents anything, as if the given were missing. On the contrary, he resists this excess, until it gives up its visibility to him (as one makes restitution). Rothko resists what he received as a violent given—too violent for anyone but him—by phenomenalizing it on the screen of spread-out color: "I have imprisoned the most utter violence in every square inch of their [the paintings'] surface" (qtd. in Breslin 358). What is true of art is true of literature and of all speculative thinking: the immense effort to resist the given as long as the given-to can endure it, in order to phenomenalize the given. Genius consists only in a great resistance to the impact of the given. In every case, the phenomenon, which has the character of an event, takes the shape of the revealed—that is, it phenomenalizes the given-to through the same movement by which the given-to forces that which gives *itself* to show *itself* a bit more.

The revealed is neither a deep layer nor a particular region of phenomenality, but the universal mode of phenomenalization of that which gives *itself* in what shows *itself*. At the same time, it establishes the originary evential character of every phenomenon insofar as it gives *itself* before showing *itself*. The time has come, then, to raise a final question: does not the universality of the phenomenon as event, and so as a given brought to manifestation as revelation by and for a given-to, definitively abolish, de jure if not de facto, the caesura that metaphysics has unceasingly hollowed out between the world of supposedly constituted, producible, and repeatable—and thus exclusively rational—objects, on the one hand, and the world of the revealed of Revelation, the world of events neither constitutible, nor repeatable, nor immediately producible and so supposedly irrational, on the other? This caesura was imposed at the moment when the doctrine of the object attempted (successfully) to reduce the question and the field of phenomenality to purely apparent phenomena, deprived of the *self*, devalued as a being and equally as a certitude. As soon as phenomenology knew how to reopen the field of phenomenality, to include in it objects as specific cases of phenomena (impoverished and common law) and surround them with the immense region of saturated phenomena, this caesura was no longer justified. Or, rather, it becomes a denial of phenomenality, itself irrational and ideological. If we admit that this caesura has no right to be, what consequences follow? That the givens retrieved by Revelation—in this instance, the unique Jewish and Christian Revelation—must be read and treated as legitimate phenomena, subject to the same operations as those that result from the givens of the world: reduction to the given, eventiality, reception by the given-to, resistance, saturated phenomena, progression of the transmutation of what gives *itself* into what shows *itself*, and so on. Undoubtedly, such a phenomenological place of theology necessitates (and already has) very particular protocols, conforming to the exceptional phenomena that are in question. For example, the event can have the form of a miracle, the given becomes the election and the promise, resistance of the given-to is deepened in the conversion of the witness, transmutation of what gives *itself* into what shows *itself* requires theological virtues, its progressivity is extended in the eschatological return of the Ruler, and so on. I have neither the authority nor the competence to follow up on these. But I have the right to call them to the attention of theologians. They must cease to reduce the fundamental givens of Revelation (Creation, Resurrection, miracles, divinization, etc.) to objectifying models that more or less repeat the human sciences. For the same phenomenality applies to all givens, from the most impoverished (formalisms, mathematics), to those of common law (physical sciences, technical objects), to saturated phenomena (event, idol, flesh, icon), including the possibility of phenomena that combine these four types of saturation (the phenomena of Revelation).

TRANSLATION BY BEATA STARWASKA

NOTES

1. [Ed.: Here and throughout, Marion italicizes the neuter reflexive pronoun. As he makes clear in the next paragraph, he does this to draw attention to the fact that he is exploring what it means to speak of the *self*-givenness of the phenomenon.]

2. [Ed.: In most places, *la donation* is translated as "the given." Sometimes, however, it is translated as "the donation" or "givenness."]

3. One realizes already that even the interpretation of a banal phenomenon as given not only does not prohibit hermeneutics, but requires it. This is my reply to the objections of Grondin (43–44) and Greisch.

4. [Ed.: "Il nous met en scène," literally "it puts us on the (theatrical) stage."]

5. [Ed.: Material in German in brackets is in the original. Material in French was inserted by the translator or editor.]

6. See my *Étant donné*, §§ 13–17.

7. Following the excellent formulation of Romano (96).

8. Let it be noted that I say "by giving a myself a me," and not "by giving it to me," since at the moment it gives it (to me), I am precisely not there yet to receive it.

9. [Ed.: "The given-to" is the translation for the neologism *l'adonné*, a past participle form.]

10. [Ed.: The French is *pourpre transcendantalice*, a play on words: *pourpre cardinalice* is an expression referring to the symbolic color associated with high church officials, as well as royalty and aristocracy.]

11. [Ed.: In French, the developer, a chemical used to make the image on photographic paper visible, is called *le révélateur*—literally, "the revelator."]

WORKS CITED

Breslin, James. *Mark Rothko. A Biography.* Chicago: University of Chicago Press, 1993.

Descartes, Rene. *Meditations on First Philosophy.* Notre Dame, Ind.: University of Notre Dame Press, 1990.

Greisch, J. "L'herméneutique dans la 'Phénoménologie comme telle. Trois questions à propos de *Réduction et donation.'*" *Revue de Métaphysique et de Morale* 1 (1991): 43–64.

Grondin, J. "Objections à Jean-Luc Marion." *Laval Philosophique et Théologique* 43/3 (1987): 425–427.

Husserl, Edmund. *Ideas Pertaining to a Pure Phenomenology and to a Phenomenological Philosophy.* Trans. F. Kersten. In *Collected Works of Edmund Husserl*, vol. 3. Boston: Martinus Nijhoff, 1982.

———. *On the Phenomenology of the Consciousness of Internal Time.* Trans. John Barnett Brough. In *Collected Works of Edmund Husserl*, vol. 4. Boston: Kluwer Academic Publishers, 1991.

Kant, Emmanuel. *Critique of Pure Reason.* Cambridge: Cambridge University Press, 1998.

Marion, Jean-Luc. *Étant donné. Essai d'une phénoménologie de la donation.* Paris: Presses universitaires de France, 1997.

Montaigne. *The Complete Essays of Montaigne.* Trans. Donald Frame. Stanford, Calif.: Stanford University Press, 1958.

Romano, Claude. *L'événement et le monde.* Paris: Presses universitaires de France, 1998.

Phenomenality and Transcendence

Marlène Zarader

My essay forms part of a debate directly traceable to two books by Dominique Janicaud: *Le tournant théologique de la phénoménologie française* and *La phénoménologie éclatée*.[1] I would like to take up and clarify the following problem: whether, and under what conditions, it is possible to affirm a transcendence within a strictly philosophical discourse, in particular when this discourse claims to be phenomenological. I will seek this clarification through a consideration of several questions.

First: Why does this possibility appear to be problematic? In other words, why might philosophy in general (including phenomenology) seem in principle to be unable to embrace transcendence?

Second: On the basis of what renewal does a certain contemporary, and in particular French, phenomenology believe itself capable of surpassing these limits and opening itself to some transcendence?

Third, and finally: To what degree do these attempts succeed? It is here that the question of the legitimacy of such attempts arises—the only question raised by Janicaud. Do they manage to make good on their claim—namely, to give an account of a transcendence inscribed in phenomenality itself? And, if these attempts do not succeed—if, as Janicaud maintains, they cannot succeed without encountering insurmountable methodological contradictions—then it will be necessary to ask whether such an account is in general possible. Is it possible—or is it radically out of the question—to show a transcendence demanding recognition within experience.

These three axes of questioning will guide my reflection.

I

First: philosophy's inability to embrace transcendence.

1. To begin with, how should we understand the term *transcendence*? As long as transcendence was characterized as a being, albeit a supreme being, it got along very well with philosophy. The idea of a conflict between the two—that is, of resistance to transcendence on the part of the thought attempting to grasp it—is not without origin. This idea presupposes a certain understanding of philosophy and also of transcendence—in other words, a significant effort of redefinition.

A redefinition of *philosophy*: philosophy must be assigned its proper limits —assigned, that is, to the event, to the impossibility of escaping the determination of beings as presence. From this point of view, philosophy indeed succeeds in going beyond beings, but only in the direction of the "what" of beings; thus, philosophy can in no way deal with that which absents itself absolutely.

A redefinition of *transcendence*: It must be the case that certain "realities" (whatever their exact identity; it may have to do with being, or God, or the Other) withdraw from all presence, that they be given only in this withdrawal. These are the realities that will thus be named "transcendent" in the precise sense that, by the very fact of excluding themselves from the order of presence, they overflow the limits of philosophy, defined as it is by that order.

This is the double condition required in order for the relationship of philosophy to transcendence to take the form of a problem. This double condition was obviously established by Heidegger and inherited by his successors. In effect, it was Heidegger who identified philosophy with metaphysics, understood as the metaphysics of presence, at the same time that he pointed to a *difference* that sustains metaphysics, but that metaphysics never accounts for: thus he called our attention both to presence and to what is other than presence. On this basis it became possible to deplore philosophy's inability to envision a radical alterity, an alterity that nonetheless persists in calling upon us; and thus it also became possible to appeal to the necessity of renewing thought, in such a way as to enable it to embrace that which it had previously grasped only by disfiguring it.

This very general structure, the origins of which are found in Heidegger, are found again, in various forms, in a number of ways of thinking that characterize modernity. I will consider two of the many possible examples.

First, in the work of Heidegger himself: that which resists in this way (resists presence, as well as the philosophy associated with presence), and which thus finds itself in the position of the wholly other is first of all being. To be sure, being cannot be separated from beings, but neither is being reducible to beings; it is defined precisely by its difference, and it is in this sense that one can designate it as "transcendent par excellence" (as Heidegger does in *Being and Time*, section 7).

On the other hand, the supposed transcendence of God in theology is not transcendence in the sense just defined (the sense of a truly radical alterity, of an excess with respect to presence), since, according to the Heideggerian analysis, the God of theology remains a being. God is thus situated within metaphysical thought (which is constituted at the outset as onto-theo-logy), but only because he has lost his transcendence—in other words, because he has already ceased to be God.

This is to say that, in the Heideggerian view, the transcendence of being escapes ontology, just as the transcendence of God escapes theology. In the onto-theo-logical framework of metaphysics, no authentic transcendence can find a place.

A second illustration: Levinas. Here the inability of philosophy to think transcendence understood as radical excess with respect to presence is faulted in another vocabulary, with a view to a different intellectual objective, and yet by a very similar form of argument.

First, consider the analogies. The whole history of philosophy, dominated by ontology, is presented by Levinas as a "philosophy of the same" (*Découvrant* 188; my translation), stricken from the beginning with an "insurmountable allergy" to alterity (ibid.). To be sure, it is concerned with the Other, but it cannot encounter it without losing it irremediably *as* Other. Is this to say that the Other cannot be found? It can be, but not where philosophy had always looked (that is, in ontology), but where it was always overlooked (that is, in ethics): "The absolutely Other is the other person" (*Totalité* 9; my translation).

We see that, in Levinas as in Heidegger, Western thought as a whole is confronted with that which escapes it and which nevertheless never ceases to lay claim upon us: "something" resists the ascendancy of the same, interrupting or disturbing the order of presence, preventing this order from resting peacefully in itself. This something is precisely irreducible to any thing, and presents itself as absolutely Other. The great difference, of course, is that whereas Heidegger designates this absolute Other as being, Levinas recognizes it as the other person.

The problem is therefore to know in what precise sense the other person can be understood as *wholly Other*. Levinas's answer is well known; the other person is the Other, provided he or she is not reduced to the familiar *alter ego*, but is finally recognized in his or her irreducibility—that is, as the face. Now, the face is the site of the irruption of transcendence in phenomenality. It is that which, in presence, exceeds all presence—since it bears the trace of God. In pursuing this trace, Levinas ascends from the order of the same to the wholly

Other which absolutely escapes this order, in the sense that it no longer allows itself to be assimilated into it.

What arises from this double analysis? That philosophy has no access to transcendence, whether transcendence is understood as being, as God, or as the Other. A fundamental closure of philosophy makes it, in principle, unable to grasp transcendence, insofar as this is understood according to the category of an excess with respect to presence.

2. Let us now take a second step that will likewise be divided into two parts. First, in what way are these limits, understood as limits of philosophy in its entirety, applicable to *phenomenology*? Second, in what way does phenomenology itself seem to contain the promise of surpassing these limits?

The answer to the first question is now almost a commonplace. It was outlined by Heidegger, elaborated by Jacques Derrida, taken up and illustrated by Jean-Luc Marion. It consists in saying that phenomenology, as established by Husserl, "reproduces the metaphysical determination of presence" (Marion, *Réduction* 8) and therefore remains vulnerable to the same criticism as that just developed.

But, in this view, the adherence to metaphysics would not be necessary to phenomenology *as such*: it would indicate simply that the privilege accorded to intuition by Husserl led him to a restrictive understanding of the phenomenon. This would leave entirely intact the possibility of another phenomenology that would no longer be guided in its apprehension of the phenomenon by the sole category of objectivity. Thus escaping the fascination of presence (to which Husserl was still subject), this other phenomenology might prove capable of doing justice to a nonobjective giving. It could thus embrace what had previously been designated by the term *transcendence*.

The problem is to know why phenomenology might, more or better than other forms of philosophy, recognize the claim of transcendence. The answer is clear: if this transcendence insists on giving itself to us (as was assumed at the outset, in the very framing of the problem), then it must be possible to take one's bearings by this giving—that is, finally to elaborate a set of concepts that are faithful to it, rather than misrepresenting it. The elaboration of this set of concepts will undoubtedly require a redefinition of certain Husserlian concepts (in the first place, that of the phenomenon), but it will be undertaken in *the name of phenomenality itself*, since it will aim at embracing in discourse that which demands attention in experience. On the contrary, strict faithfulness to Husserlian concepts would betray phenomenality, because Husserl's procedure consisted of subjecting the phenomenon to restrictive conditions. Husserl wanted every appearing to take the form of an object, which blinded him to the excess that nonetheless is traced at the heart of the appearing itself, and that thus demands to be thought—albeit against Husserl, and at the price of a reordering of his inaugural concepts.

In short, if phenomenology can, better than other philosophies, do justice to transcendence, this is because the only authority that it recognizes is experience. Now, it is the case that transcendence is inscribed within experience. Therefore, insofar as phenomenology remains faithful to this authority alone (without adding any metaphysical assumption to it), it will be able to embrace what philosophy, because of these very assumptions, had been condemned to ignore or to refuse.

II

This brings me to the second axis of this analysis: the attempts to give an account of the very excess of transcendence within a phenomenological discourse, attempts that Janicaud takes to task. Given the impossibility of examining all of them, I will limit myself to two: Levinas and Marion.

Let us first specify the general meaning of these attempts. Clearly one is confronted here with an alternative: either these forms of discourse *affirm* a transcendence, thus proceeding dogmatically, and they will be hard-pressed to show how they are legitimated; or, far from *positing* a transcendence, they find its mark on the very phenomena themselves. It is only in the latter case that these forms of discourse can remain phenomenological and benefit at the same time, as do all rigorous phenomenological forms of discourses, from a legitimation by experience.

It is therefore the second alternative that is taken up by the authors who are of interest to us. The problem is to know if they in fact succeed in holding to it. And the only way to decide this is to consider what would be necessary for them to do so. By their own admission, the success of their attempt in effect implies several conditions—which seem to be contradictory.

The first condition: in order for this discourse not to betray (as do all the earlier forms that it finds fault with) *that* of which it claims to speak, the transcendent must preserve its full transcendence, its pure alterity—irrelative, unconditioned, self-signifying. Now, transcendence can preserve its purity only if it proves to be irreducible to any *object* (which is always the correlate of an envisioning) as well as to any *subject* (which is always the giver of meaning). This is to say that the transcendent can preserve or obtain the intended status only if it goes beyond what canonical phenomenology has recognized as the conditions of the possibility of *experience* itself.

At the same time, however, and this is the second requirement, it is necessary that the transcendent give itself and that I receive it, and thus that it be inscribed within an experience.

It thus seems that we are at an impasse; to remain fully transcendent, the transcendent must lay claim upon us as unbounded by experience, but to retain the status of a phenomenon, it must be situated within experience.

How will our authors succeed in holding together this double requirement? By preserving the two poles of experience, but under *erasure*—that is, by emptying them as radically as possible. Thus the recourse to two tightly joined concepts (which prove to be absolutely unavoidable from such a perspective, and which we therefore find in all the relevant bodies of thought): the concept of *nothingness* (on the side of the object) and that of *passivity* (on the side of the subject).

On the side of the object, in order for the given truly to escape presence, that given must not only not have the form of an object, but it must be no being whatsoever: it must be other than any being, an absolute nonbeing—a nothing. On the side of the subject, for that which is given to radiate in its virgin alterity, I must not lay hold of it, but let it lay hold of me. In order for the scales to tilt to the side of this free givenness, without being in any way conditioned (and therefore disfigured) by me, subjectivity must efface and hollow itself out to the point of becoming totally passive: a pure pole of reception that would no longer be "constituting." Such is the double gesture carried out by each of our authors. However, once again, the model or matrix of this gesture is already found in Heidegger.

We will thus begin with Heidegger, who initiates the first gesture with *Being and Time*, the second after the turn.

In section 44 of *Being and Time*, and especially in the lecture "What is Metaphysics?" of 1929, Heidegger endeavors to describe the phenomenal givenness of the Other of every being, which he calls the nothing. His project is then to assure, by way of the nothing, an access to being itself. As Marion has shown (*Réduction* 249–302), it is not certain that in 1927 and 1929 Heidegger succeeded in justifying this interpretation of the nothing as being. On the other hand, by the analysis of anxiety, he did in fact establish that the nothing is given, that we can encounter it in an experience. Thus he succeeded in securing the status of the appearing of a phenomenon that no longer has the form of an object (which Husserl would have judged to be impossible).

After the turn, the powers (especially the powers of decision) that *Being and Time* still accorded to *Dasein* are progressively depleted, to the advantage of the ever more insistent theme of letting-be. To be sure, Heidegger always maintained, even in his latest work, the affirmation of an interdependence between man and being, but within this interdependence being gains preeminence; humankind is not the master of being, it is not the origin of its givenness, it does not decide even its meaning. At most it can provide being a welcoming space, and it can do this provided that it abandons itself to that which claims it. Such is *Gelassenheit*, an originary passivity that "lets" being be, and which thus can embrace without misrepresenting the pure "gift" of being.

In making being a nothing and man its shepherd, Heidegger, I have said, outlined a matrix. Levinas and Marion were to inherit and radicalize this structure.

How does this structure appear in Levinas? On the one hand, the Other is clearly thought as a nothing with regard to beings. To be sure, in *Totality and Infinity*, the face remains, in some way, a being. But it is an incomparable being, which "reveals the infinite" (*Totalité* 188; my translation), which "proceeds from the absolutely absent" (*Découvrant* 198) and thus overflows the very field in which it is inscribed. And *Otherwise than Being* goes further still in this gesture of tearing away from what Levinas calls essence, in taking his bearings toward "a pre-original, an unrepresentable, an invisible" (*Autrement* 112)—and by that very fact an irreducible "enigma." The Other as thought by the late Levinas not only cannot be contained by the category of beings, but invites us to go "beyond being."

On the other hand, subjectivity is literally extenuated, emptied of all initiative and even all consistency, fully exposed to the abrupt irruption of the Other. This is the best-known and most constant aspect of Levinas's thought. It had already begun to emerge in the very first texts—for example, *De l'existence à l'existant* (where the subject appeared as captivated, possessed, invaded, submerged, given over, etc.; see 73, 94, 96, etc.). Later, it is precisely the exposure to the Other and the extreme passivity that this presupposes that properly defined subjectivity, which were then described as "more passive than all passivity," called upon entirely from without, exposed to a transcendence that, in laying claim to the subject, constitutes it as subject.

Finally, in the case of Marion, we can see the same structure at work, even as its purpose appears still more clearly than elsewhere, because it is here made explicit. Let us first examine the structure itself.

On the one hand, once liberated from the limits that confined the phenomenon, the phenomenon is clearly presented, apart from any object and even any being, as that which overflows, exceeds, or saturates. The only means for letting it be in its excess is to take its givenness alone as a rule, a givenness that itself is reduced to the pure "form" of the "call." The phenomenon will thus be everything that, in being given, lays claim upon me.

On the other hand, and in return, to be able to receive this gift in its purity, the subject, itself cast wholly outside the domain of being, must be nothing other than the "laid-claim-to." It is this subjectivity wholly summoned outside itself, "compelled to alterity" (*Réduction* 300), that *Reduction and Donation* names the *Interloqué*, "the called up short" (300). The book that followed, *Étant donné*, takes up the analysis and develops it, by making of this expropriated subject not that which constitutes the phenomenon, but that which is dispossessed by it. It is therefore called the *Attributaire* (the "beneficiary" or "allottee"), understood now not as a subject having the experience of an object, but as a witness stricken by powerlessness who has "the counter-experience of a non-object" (*Étant* 300).

Why does Marion set up this paradoxical pair of the gift and its beneficiary? This is where we see the ultimate purpose of his approach. In effect, his response includes two closely related levels. The reasons he proceeds in this way are the following: First, to reverse the polarity of phenomenality to the sole benefit of the phenomenon. The point is to justify the possibility of the phenomenon's appearing "as itself, of itself and from itself" (*Étant* 305). Second, for phenomenality, thus redefined and enlarged, to be able to include within itself, in the status of a "possible figure" (*Étant* 326), the phenomenon of Revelation—understood as the revelation of Christ.

Let me emphasize that this strategy is in no way clandestine. Marion announces it openly. To do justice phenomenologically to the possibility of the revelation of Christ is not, for him, a heavy-handed move, since all his previous work consisted precisely in redefining phenomenality in such a way as not to exclude this possibility. In other words, if the phenomenon is *always* and in its very essence an excess, if what is given by it is always a radical alterity that imposes itself on me and lays claim to me, then nothing excludes the possibility that it might give also and first of all this Other exemplar who is Christ.

Having examined these two illustrations (Levinas and Marion), we can now return to the structure that they have in common. We have seen that the paradoxical "object" whose givenness is to be guaranteed is, in each case, emptied of all subsistence as well as all consistency, even as the "subject" that must receive this giving is, for its part, emptied of all power and initiative. Why is this structure set up; what advantage is expected from it? Its purpose is to allow the appearing, outside of any decision I might take—and even outside of all constituting in the phenomenological sense of the term—of a Wholly Other that imposes itself upon me. This Other will thus give itself in a relationship (since it gives itself to me) without losing anything of its complete otherness (since this me is no longer anything): there will be a *pure* or *absolute*—that is, nonrelative—experience. And it is imperative that experience be pure (not contaminated by me) in order for otherness to remain intact. Such is the wager, clearly discerned by Janicaud (as it had been earlier by Derrida, in his remarkable article on Levinas ["Violence"]), and something that Janicaud regards to be a square circle. *If* such a pure experience is possible (but only on this condition), then one can say that a transcendence is indeed imposed on me within phenomenality, while losing nothing of its transcendence. But is such a pure experience possible, even at the limit?

III

This brings me to the third question: To what degree are these attempts successful?

This amounts to asking to what exact degree phenomenality can overflow itself intrinsically, so as to testify to what exceeds it. Are the two opposing requirements presented in the preceding part only apparently contradictory (as Levinas and Marion would have it), or are they really contradictory in the final analysis (as Janicaud maintains)?

To answer this question I will again proceed in two parts. On the one hand, I will try to discern the exact limit of these different attempts—that is, the prohibition they transgress that cannot, in my view, be transgressed. On the other hand, once this prohibition is recognized, it will still be necessary to ask whether a (noncontradictory) possibility remains for making room for transcendence and, if so, in what such a possibility might consist.

1. The first point: the limit of these attempts. The problem, you will recall, is to know whether, without leaving the ground of phenomenology, one can think a pure experience, in a sense that does without the double category of the object and the subject. To anticipate my answer, I will say that it is indeed possible to think without contradiction an experience without object, but that the same is not true for an experience without subject. Let us consider each of these two statements.

One can think an experience without object, because to do so is to bypass *one* determination of the phenomenon (its Husserlian determination), but not *every* possible determination of the phenomenon. This is clear in Heidegger, who, it seems to me, succeeds in what he sets out to do, and this without contradiction, as is shown, notably, by his analysis of anxiety. This analysis remains fully phenomenological—ordered by the description of a lived experience— while bringing to light the paradoxical appearance of what is "nothing" and "nowhere." One could doubtless show as well that the case of the analysis of the work of art is not very different: the Greek temple or the poem brings the invisible as such to the visible; it brings to appearing the very thing that withdraws, and as withdrawn. This idea of a phenomenalization of absence cannot purely and simply be set aside; its legitimacy is based on experience itself. Indeed, it is not even foreign to Husserl: despite the commitment to objectivism that he always held to, he knew to give a place, however marginal, to a nonobjectifying form of intentionality, and therefore to an "intentionality without object," to use Rudolf Bernet's expression (327).

Still, this same Bernet arrives at a very different conclusion where the *subject* is concerned. Even as he endeavors to show the extremely nuanced and complex character of the determination of the subject proposed by Husserl, he concludes his inquiry with the affirmation that it is impossible to recognize in Husserl's work an "intentionality without a subject" (327). However one redefines the subject, it remains central to Husserl's project.

It seems to me that there is no getting around this conclusion and that one must go even further: subjectivity may well be redefined, but it remains the living nerve of every *phenomenological* project. If one attempts to slice through this nerve, the whole strategy crumbles. And, as a matter of fact, all the attempts (and there are many of them) that have been undertaken, in the framework of phenomenology, to be done with subjectivity have not been able to avoid smuggling it in through the back door. Such is the case with Levinas (as Derrida has shown), such is the case with Sartre (in *La transcendance de l'égo*), and such, finally and paradigmatically, is the case with Marion.

In order not to overburden this essay, I will limit myself to this last example. We have seen that Marion endeavors to assign everything to the unconditioned givenness of the phenomenon. This brings him logically to want to have done with the subject, understood as a constituting subject. In effect, if the subject constitutes the phenomenon—if it permits it to appear, and to appear according to such and such a meaning—then one can no longer say that this phenomenon shows itself *of* itself, or that it signifies *by* itself. And since Marion's ambition is precisely to guarantee this self-signification, he works at "radically dispossessing" subjectivity.

By what means does he hope to accomplish this dispossession? By "turning" the subject around, by "reversing" it to make of it an instance that is entirely empty, passive, seized upon, affected, powerless, and so on. Such indeed, we have seen, is the definition of the witness.

As Janicaud has observed, the problem is that to reverse the subject is obviously not at all to suppress it, but, quite to the contrary, to maintain it. One can vary as one pleases the characteristics attributed to the subject (by privileging its being-affected rather than its active being, for example), yet its *function* (which is to allow the appearing of phenomena) remains unchanged. However, if this function remains unchanged, it means that the character of subjectivity is maintained throughout, and that the promised dispossession or dismissal has not taken place.

Marion thus takes up with one hand what he seemed to abandon with the other, *all the while denying having taken it up.* This is his inconsistency. To be clear: by insisting on the powerlessness of the witness, he seems to deprive the witness of all the powers of the subject; but since he grants the witness the function of "filter" of phenomena (a filter meant to assure the possibility of their manifestation), he reestablishes, without admitting it, what he claims to have dismissed. Thus Marion has no right to affirm at the end of his last work, "The phenomenology of givenness has done with—in our view for the first time—the subject and all its recent avatars" (*Étant* 441).

The same thing could be shown in the case of Levinas—who, by striving to make the subject passive, would also like to convince us, or himself, that it no longer plays any role in the springing up of alterity. In every case, the aporia is identical. Contemporary phenomenology, especially French phenomenology, always wants to break with subjectivity to provide a clear space for a privileged givenness, which is then supposed to shine from itself, in its pure alterity. However, in order to preserve the benefit of a phenomenological justification for this givenness—in other words, in order that it indeed be a matter of *givenness*, and not of an arbitrary metaphysical postulation—these thinkers cannot do without a pole allowing the appearance of phenomena. Thus, they reintroduce surreptitiously the constitutive instance that they claimed to evacuate. Janicaud is on solid ground to see in this an insurmountable contradiction.

What is the upshot of this analysis? It implies that one can push back the limits that Husserl assigned to phenomenology very far—but only to a certain point. It is this point that I have endeavored to discern. There is nothing illegitimate in maintaining that the Other whose givenness one wishes to assure exceeds the form of the object and even of beings, since this excess does not prevent the Other from being inscribed within phenomenality. But

Levinas and Marion go further still: they want to radically sever this givenness from any constituting pole, and that is the prohibition that one cannot breach without seeing the very ground of phenomenology slip away. To want the phenomenon to appear *absolutely*, without reference to any instance that can guarantee its appearing, is to condemn oneself to losing it *as* phenomenon; and to deprive oneself, as a result, of all justification by phenomenality.

This, I believe, is what Heidegger understood. Initiating the redefinition of the phenomenon, Heidegger went *as far as possible* in the direction of a self-givenness: the phenomenon gives itself by itself, of itself, and the nothing itself can be given in this way. But Heidegger knew not to go *too* far, since he took into account the instance in which this given finds its space of welcome and nomination. This instance is *Dasein. Dasein* is emptied of everything that might give "consistency" to the traditional subject while preserving the place: Heidegger keeps only the *site* of previous subjectivity—precisely the only element that one cannot do without.

One can thus understand what makes the arch-passivity characteristic of Levinas and Marion a contradictory concept, as distinct from the Heideggerian letting-be, which was nevertheless its initial model.

The theme of letting-be invites the subject to an *abstention*, understood as a necessary condition of welcoming. Against the conceptual laying-hold-of that risks having to do only with the remains of the other, Heidegger endeavors to preserve its fragile alterity as much as possible. To preserve it is to let it unfold, to come to one's encounter, and thus to make oneself as discrete as possible, that is, to give up grasping. But this abstention evidently cannot go to the point of an *abolition*, since, if I abolished myself, I would cease at the same moment to "let" come this other with which I am so concerned. This is to say that "to let" of course means, negatively, to cease to grasp; but it also means, positively, to grant a space of appearance. The whole point of the Heideggerian approach lies in this double meaning of "to let": it is a matter of being almost absent, in order for the other to retain its own face, while not being completely absent, in order for this face to appear.

When one does not take this fragile equilibrium into account, one imposes on thought, in the name of passivity, a condition that contradicts its exercise. The tendency of certain post-Heideggerian authors to make the subject ever more passive follows from their attempt to reach the limit where it might become possible for the subject to attend, *as absent*, the rising up of what presents itself, which, owing to this absence, would finally present itself purely. A square circle, Janicaud would say. And this verdict, far from being applicable to Heidegger, is confirmed by him: if thought wishes to embrace anything, even a nothing, it necessarily presupposes a *there* that guarantees the meaning of the being of this nothing, thus causing it to escape from *pure* alterity.

If this is indeed the case—if, in the framework of phenomenality, one cannot do without a pole that guarantees the meaning of the phenomenon—then the transcendence of which this pole is a witness can only be relative: transcendence in immanence, an other for me. The phantasm of a *pure* or *absolute* alterity proves to be unachievable. Unachievable in phenomenology.

What conclusion should be drawn from this concerning the relationship of phenomenality and transcendence? Here we must avoid mistaking the lessons to be learned. Does it follow that because transcendence is relative, it is not transcendent, and that the subject, because it is maintained, remains all-powerful? In other words, do the difficulties encountered by the different attempts studied here force us to return to a more traditional approach in which thought, condemned to move within the circle of immanence, would renounce embracing that which overflows this circle? I believe that this is not the case, and this leads me to the final point of this analysis: the perspectives.

2. It seems to me that the only way to think without contradiction a transcendence traced within immanence itself is to think it as that which disturbs or unsettles the order of phenomena, but without ever being separable from them—that is, without ever becoming a *pure* transcendence. And the only concept, if there is one, that might allow us to give up the phantasm of purity is the concept of *subversion*.

This is a concept that I borrow from Roland Barthes, a source far from all phenomenology. To speak as he does of "subtle subversion" (*Plaisir* 74) is to distinguish subversion from all destruction. Destruction dreams of purity: it wants to have done with things once and for all, doubtless in order all the better to usher in something new. Subversion acknowledges its own impurity and interminability: it knows it can never extract itself from the place that it contests; nevertheless, it strives continuously to upset and to divert that place. As we know, Barthes wishes for a subversion of language: he shows that to combat "canonical language" (15) is not to leave it behind—because no one can, except by being reduced to silence—but to undermine it from the inside.

This gesture loses none of its effectiveness in being transposed to the field of phenomenology.[2] As with language, the strict realm of immanence can be unsettled or subverted; not only can it be, but it is at every moment. To affirm this is in no way to leave this realm, but to remain uncomfortably in it and to recognize this discomfort as a law. No transcendent is able to appear, in the sense of revealing itself in its Glory. But it is possible to "let" immanence manifest everything that disturbs it. This can be conveyed in a double register:

On the one hand, there is doubtless nothing but objects and beings, and yet everything happens as if these beings, in presenting themselves as unsettled (for example in anxiety, or in other limit-experiences), let us glimpse their own margin.

On the other hand, and above all, in a still more radical manner, there is subjectivity—an unavoidable subjectivity, required imperatively in order to speak of the field of phenomena; but this must be thought as the place of a perpetual *crisis*, an infinite *perturbation*. This is the only means to dispossess the subject *in its presence*.

To conclude, then, I will say that there is no "pure experience." No Revelation, with a capital R, can be given within phenomenality. To postulate such a Revelation is, as Janicaud says, in effect to bring about a metaphysical overstepping of the phenomenal sphere. What, then, is the given? Nothing but immanence, nothing but a fragile, precarious, ever-threatened immanence. To think without contradiction the "and" in the copula "phenomenality and transcendence" presupposes abandoning all hope of a pure revelation of the transcendent in the phenomenal, in favor of an approach concerned with phenomenality's entry into crisis, with no outside discernible other than this crisis itself. And it is within this internal trembling of immanence that the possibility of transcendence remains as a hollow inscription—a transcendence that can function only, in phenomenological discourse, as a *critical*, and never positive, possibility. And perhaps this would be one dimension, or one of the possible readings (the most fecund, in my eyes), of Levinas's work.

From this perspective, we find the conditions of experience and appearing unsettled, but not challenged, by certain givings. The recourse to the concept of subversion seemed to me to be a way to hold off two dangers that threaten phenomenology: the first danger is to want at all costs to *maintain* the conditions of experience, as they have been set forth by Husserl, at the risk of limiting the amplitude of the field of phenomena; the second, and opposite, danger is to want to *suppress* these conditions, at the risk of seeing the field of phenomena disappear. In phenomenology as elsewhere, purity is always dangerous or naive.

TRANSLATION BY RALPH HANCOCK, JOHN HANCOCK, AND
NATHANIEL HANCOCK

NOTES

1. The first of these has been translated into English in *Theological Turn*.
2. Or, yet, to other fields. I am thinking of a remarkable article by Moutot, who rereads the fiction of Echenoz in the light of concepts borrowed from Barthes. See Moutot, "L'équipée."

WORKS CITED

Barthes, Roland. *Le Plaisir du texte*. Paris: Minuit, 1973. Translated as *The Pleasure of the Text*. Trans. Richard Miller. New York: Hill and Wang, 1975.
Bernet, Rudolf. *La Vie du sujet*. Paris: Presses universitaires de France, 1994.
Derrida, Jacques. "Violence et métaphysique." In J. Derrida, *L'Écriture et la différence*, 117–228. Paris: Minuit, 1967.
Heidegger, Martin. *Sein und Zeit*. Tubingen: Niemeyer, 1927. Translated as *Being and Time*. Trans. Joan Stambaugh. Albany: SUNY Press, 1969.
Janicaud, Dominique. *La Phénoménologie éclatée*. Paris: l'Éclat, 1998.

——. *Le tournant théologique de la phénoménologie française.* Paris: l'Éclat, 1991. Translated as *The Theological Turn in French Phenomenology.* Trans. Bernard G. Prusack. In Dominique Janicaud, Jean-François Courtine, Jean-Louis Chrétien, Michel Henry, Jean-Luc Marion, and Paul Ricoeur, *Phenomenology and the "Theological Turn": The French Debate,* trans. Bernard G. Prusak, Jeffrey L. Kosky, and Thomas A. Carlson, 16–103. New York: Fordham University Press, 2000.

Levinas, Emmanuel. *Autrement qu'être ou Au-delà de l'essence.* 2nd ed. The Hague: Martinus Nijhoff, 1974. Translated as *Otherwise than Being or Beyond Essence.* Trans. Alphonso Lingis. The Hague: Martinus Nijhoff, 1981.

——. *En découvrant l'existence avec Husserl et Heidegger.* 2nd ed. 1947. Reprint, Paris, Vrin: 1967. Translated as *Discovering Existence with Husserl and Heidegger.* Trans. and ed. Richard A. Cohen and Michael B. Smith. Evanston: Northwestern University Press, 1998.

——. *De l'existence à l'existant,* 2nd ed. 1947. Reprint, Paris: Vrin, 1977. Translated as *Existence and Existents.* Trans. Alphonso Lingis. Dordrecht: Kluwer Academic Publishers, 1988.

——. *Totalité et infini.* The Hague: Nijhoff, 1961. Translated as *Totality and Infinity.* Trans. Alphonso Lingis. Pittsburgh: Duquesne University Press, 1969.

Marion, Jean-Luc. *Étant donné, Essai d'une phénoménologie de la donation.* Paris: Presses universitaires de France, 1997.

——. *Réduction et donation, Recherches sur Husserl, Heidegger et la phénoménologie.* Paris: Presses universitaires de France, 1989. Translated as *Reduction and Givenness: Investigations of Husserl, Heidegger, and Phenomenology.* Trans. Thomas A. Carlson. Evanston: Northwestern University Press, 1998.

Moutot, Gilles. "L'équipée lente. Roland Barthes et Theodor W. Adorno, lecteurs imaginaires de Jean Echenoz." *La Manchette. Revue de littérature comparée* 1 (Spring 2000): 197–232.

Sartre, Jean-Paul. *La transcendance de l'égo; esquisse d'une description phénoménologique.* 1936. Reprint, Paris: Vrin, 1966. Translated as *The Transcendence of the Ego: An Existential Theory of Consciousness.* Trans. Forest Williams and Robert Kirkpatrick. New York: Noonday Press, 1957.

Transcendence and the Hermeneutic Circle

Some Thoughts on Marion and Heidegger

Béatrice Han

Although there has been a considerable debate around Jean-Luc Marion's writings on phenomenology (in particular about intuition and donation) in the last ten years or so,[1] comparatively less critical attention has been devoted to his earlier articles published under the title of *God Without Being*. Although my main concern is not theology, these texts are interesting to me for two reasons. First, they assume a Heideggerian background against which the question of the meaning and limits of Heidegger's phenomenological rein- terpretation of transcendence is brought to the fore. Indeed, the main ele- ments of Heidegger's conceptual framework are endorsed from the start[2]—the definition of *Dasein* as being-in-the-world, the ontological difference, the al- ethic structure of being (as allowing phenomena to be disclosed only on the background of its own withdrawal), the interpretation of metaphysics and its history as the repeated forgetting of both this difference and this structure. In this context, phenomenological transcendence (as the defining characteristic of *Dasein*)[3] becomes the problematic core of Marion's criticism of Heidegger's alleged failure to think the manifestation of the divine and our relationship to it by means of two successive reductions: First, being is identified as the necessary horizon of any understanding of God: thus, "the truth about 'God' can only come from that from which truth itself comes, in other words, from being, its constellation and its openness" (*Without* 41, translation modified [F65]). Second, being itself is referred to *Dasein* as its condition of possibility:

> To say "Being/*Sein*" quite simply would not be possible if man were not able to attain his dignity of Dasein; Dasein here indicates what is peculiar to the human being, which consists in the fact that, in his being, not only *its* being is an issue (as *Sein und Zeit* repeats in 1927), but more essentially, as Heidegger says in 1928, Being itself and its comprehension. (*Without* 42 [F66])

Therefore, for Marion the main reason why Heidegger cannot think God properly is that being and, ultimately, human transcendence have become the measure of the divine, which, conversely, finds itself reduced to a mere phenomenon: "Being offers in advance the screen on which any 'God' that would be constituted would be projected and would appear—since, by definition, to be constituted signifies to be constituted as a being" (*Without* 70 [F105]). According to Marion, Heidegger's very awareness of the ontological difference, instead of allowing him to avoid the former confusions of onto-theology, paradoxically ends up being the crucial factor in his incapacity to think and relate to the sacred authentically, as the need to preserve the ontological preeminence of being leads him to repeat the metaphysical identification of God with an (ontic) entity: "Every non-metaphysical possibility of 'God' finds itself governed from the start by the thesis (hypothesis, impediment [*hypothèque*]?) of being that will accommodate it only as a being" (*Without* 70 [F105]). Consequently, the allegedly restrictive character of Heidegger's understanding of being is denounced by Marion as metaphysical, a diagnosis that rests on the ultimate dependence of being on *Dasein*'s transcendence; anthropocentrism would thus be the unthought of Heidegger's reflection on the sacred, and its downfall.

To remedy this, Marion introduces a seminal distinction between two modes of disclosure, the "idol" and the "icon," a distinction meant to overcome the primacy of human transcendence and the limitations of the ontological difference (itself understood as idolatrous)[4] by allowing a nonanthropomorphizing and nonrestrictive access to the divine. However, before reconstructing Marion's argument and turning to a critical discussion of his reading of Heidegger and of the "solution" that he suggests, I would like to outline the second reason why *God Without Being* interests me. Although the book is explicitly focused on the relations between God and being, the debate that it opens can and should be cast in terms that exceed the religious field: it bears on the conditions of possibility of phenomenality itself and their relationship to human transcendence. Indeed, Marion's attacks against Heidegger are driven mostly by what he sees as the unduly closed and overwhelming character of being as the horizon of all intelligibility, and also by his claim that this horizon would ultimately be generated by, or at least coextensive to, *Dasein*. In asserting provocatively that "God is not and does not have to be" (*Without* 3 [F12]) and that this divine freedom from the constraints of the hermeneutic circle is precisely what allows for a fuller understanding of donation and of the gift,[5] and conversely of what it means to be human, Marion is thus criticizing Heidegger for having ruled out from the start the possibility of thinking the divine as that which, by definition, escapes human intelligibility. However, the argument can be generalized if one takes it to mean that the ontological anteriority of being over any ontic manifestation excludes the possibility of *anything* showing up that would distort or exceed the space of disclosure thus opened. Such a generalization is provided by Marion himself in "The Saturated Phenomenon," in which the author defines the "saturated phenomenon," according to the Kantian table of categories, as one that is "impossible to aim at according to quantity, unbearable according to quality, but also *unconditioned, freed [ab-solu] from any horizon and irreducible to the I according to modality*" (198, my translation, my italics [F122])[6]—all characteristics that clearly apply to the divine in *God Without Being*.[7] The case of God thus becomes a particular instance of a more general difficulty,[8] that of thinking an outside to the herme-neutic circle while having to remain within it (as we are finite entities that cannot overstep our defining characteristic, namely, being-in-the-world). If, by definition, being circumscribes the scope of human intelligibility, how can anything be disclosed to us without being reduced to what we can apprehend of it? Even if phenomena are not dependent on us as subjects for their constitution (as Kant or Husserl would have it), they can appear to us only from within an understanding of Being in which we ourselves are situated and which by definition plays an enabling part (without being nothing can be *disclosed* to us) as well as a limitative one (*nothing* can be disclosed to us except on the background of being). Thus by questioning the problematic relationship be-tween God and Being, Marion is also asking a more general question:[9] What are the limits of phenomenality? Is the Heideggerian understanding of being so restrictive as to generate a complete closure of the hermeneutic circle, such that nothing could show up without being immediately reduced to an entity?

I would like to show that although Marion asks the right question, he gives the wrong answer to it. I shall proceed in two steps: First, I will show that Marion's reading of Heidegger is at best incomplete and often faulty. As we have seen, while he embraces Heidegger's analyses of onto-theology, he criticizes Heidegger's understanding of being for remaining ultimately focused on *Da-sein* as the implicit source and therefore "measure" of the hermeneutic circle: thus Heidegger himself would have unknowingly remained an idolatrous thinker. However, I shall argue that this criticism can make sense only from a non-Heideggerian perspective—in fact, a Husserlian one—and, further, that

Marion *himself* unduly restricts and anthropomorphizes Heidegger's understanding of phenomenality, thus oversimplifying considerably the relationships between transcendence, disclosure, and intelligibility. Moreover, Heidegger was much more aware than Marion suggests of the danger of hermeneutic closure; because Marion is blind to Heidegger's own attempts to deal with it, he is strangely led to unwittingly repeat some of the crucial Heideggerian moves—such as, for example, the emphasis put on *Stimmungen* and especially love (central to *What Is Called Thinking*)—which results in making his own position even more ambivalent and unstable. Second, I want to establish that even on his own terms, Marion's "solution" is invalid, mainly because it rests on an implicit contradiction between its premises (an endorsement of the phenomenological understanding of transcendence) and its conclusion (a reversion to the metaphysical conception of transcendence that ends up negating the thing in itself/phenomenon distinction by asserting the possibility for God to reveal himself unconditionally).

Let me start by bringing out the main lines of Marion's argument. *God Without Being* opens with the seminal distinction between the idol and the icon, defined as two rival "modes of visibility" and presented in a way strongly reminiscent of Heidegger's own characterization of being (as neither an entity nor a class of entities):[10] "The idol does not indicate, any more than the icon, a particular being or even class of beings. Icon and idol indicate a manner of being for beings, or at least for some of them" (7 [F15]).[11] Thus the antagonism between the idol and the icon has an ontological dimension, and presupposes a "phenomenological conflict, or rather a conflict between two phenomenologies" (ibid., translation modified). This conflict rests on two opposite understandings of phenomenality and its relationship to human disclosure. The idol, on the one hand, has two complementary characteristics. First, it opens up a pure "space of manifestation" (14 [F23]) in which the divine becomes fully visible. It is thus a superior mode of donation in the sense that it gives the phenomenon fully, without any opacity or residue (hence its dazzling quality, exemplified for Marion by the splendor of the Greek *kouroi*) (27 [F41]). However, and second, the completeness of this hyper-fulfilled donation has a flip side, which is that, conversely, the disclosed becomes dependent on and restricted by the subject's disclosive abilities—in Marion's metaphorical terms, the space of God's manifestation is measured by what the human gaze can bear of it (14 [F23]). The divine may be fully disclosed, but it cannot exceed the modalities of its disclosure. Consequently the signification and value of the idol must be reversed: its very fullness, instead of being an indicator of phenomenal richness, should be read as a "low water mark [*étiage*]" (14, 16 [F24, 27]) of the divine because the space of visibility opened up remains purely subjective, and therefore anthropomorphic: as Marion puts it, "the gaze precedes the idol because an aiming-at precedes and gives rise to that at which it aims" (11, translation modified [F19])—this anteriority being ontological, and not chronological, in that it refers the primacy of the conditions of possibility of disclosure (our aiming at the divine) over the disclosed phenomenon.

The icon, on the other hand, operates in exactly the opposite way: rather than being determined by the gaze that looks on it, and thus being transparent to that gaze, it opens up a space of manifestation that is "saturated by the invisible." The icon "attempts to render visible the invisible as such, hence to allow that the visible should never cease to refer to an other than itself" (18, translation modified [F29]). The iconic mode of (in)visibility is thus paradoxical in that it does not disclose anything but the impossibility of a complete disclosure of the divine—its irreducibility to any phenomenal manifestation, even (or especially) of the perfect kind described by the idol. This irrepresentability of the divine entails a denial of anthropocentrism pictorially symbolized by the way we are looked upon by Byzantine icons (as opposed to our gazing at Greek idols): "In the icon, the gaze of man is lost in the invisible gaze that visibly envisages him" (20 [F32]). Contrary to the idol, therefore, the icon does not disclose any phenomenon: but precisely for this reason, its signification and value must also be reversed. This impossibility should not be seen as a lack but as the sign of the icon's ontological superiority over the idol, a superiority due to the fact that it brings to the fore the nonontic dimension of the divine, and therefore shows the limits of phenomenality itself by exceeding our powers of representation.[12] In short, whereas the idol emphasizes the perfect fit between our disclosive abilities and the disclosed phenomena—and thus symbolizes the closure of the hermeneutic circle—the icon breaches this circle to indicate that, at least in the case of God, there can and must be a fundamental discrepancy between what is given and what is giving itself. Just as in the case of the Kantian sublime, the resistance of the divine to disclosure becomes in *itself* the core of the iconic donation, which thus can only work negatively by hinting at what it does not show. Because of this paradox, the icon is endowed with a fundamental "depth" and "mystery" that trigger in us a sharp awareness of our own limitations. The hubristic logic of the Copernican turn is thus defeated: instead of being comforted in our implicit trust in our disclosive powers (as in the case of idolatrous visibility, which magnifies our faculties by magnifying their object), we are de-centered and thrown beyond ourselves into an unstable state of longing and anxiety. Whereas the idol is ultimately an assertion of anthropocentrism, the icon negates the centrality of the human gaze both epistemically and morally, while conversely reasserting the ontological primacy of its impossible object over the gazed-upon subject.

Marion uses this distinction in two main ways, ways that are tightly interwoven in his text and that I will distinguish more sharply here for the sake of clarity: to condemn Heidegger's understanding of being as idolatrous, and to present his own iconic answer to the problem of the disclosure of the divine. Regarding the first point, Marion builds his definition of the idol in three steps: first, he reasserts the symbolic link established by the Platonic tradition between visibility and intelligibility, and thus shows that conceptualization itself has an idolatrous structure:

> Thus the concept on its part can take up again the characteristics of the "aesthetic" idol: because it apprehends the divine on the basis of *Dasein*, it measures the divine as a function of it; the limits of the divine experience of *Dasein* provoke a reflection both thinking and anthropomorphic mirror-effect that turns it away from aiming at, and beyond, the invisible, and allows it to freeze the divine in a concept, an invisible mirror (*Without* 29 [F44])

Indeed, for Marion the idol and the concept have the same ambivalence: On the one hand, they have the ability to encompass and thus master their object, either by fully displaying it or by exhaustively understanding its properties—as indicated by the Latin etymology of the French *com-prendre* (to take with, or within, oneself). On the other hand, in some cases, such as that of the divine or the saturated phenomena mentioned above, this very ability results in an impoverishment of the object of either vision or thought, an impoverishment symbolized by the shift from the "God of the heart" to the "God of philosophers," by which the concept of "God" "accedes to the precision that will render it operative only by remaining limited" (29 [F45]).[13] Thus, both idol and concept presuppose anthropocentrism as their hidden core: "Man remains the original locus of his idolatrous concept of the divine, because the concept marks the extreme advance, then the reflected return, of a thought that renounces venturing beyond itself, into the aiming at the invisible" (30, translation modified [F46]).

The second step in Marion's analysis consists in using this model to criticize the idolatrous character of metaphysics: "The first idolatry can be established rigorously starting from metaphysics to the extent that its essence depends on the ontological difference, but 'unthought as such' (Martin Heidegger)" (33, translation modified [F51]). This first idolatry is thus the one exposed by later Heidegger himself under the name of onto-theology, in terms that are explicitly taken up and approved without modification by Marion:

> In thinking "God" as *causa sui*, metaphysics gives itself a concept of "God" that at once marks the indisputable experience of him and his equally incontestable limitation. . . . Metaphysics indeed constructs itself in an apprehension of the transcendence of God, but only under the figure of efficiency, of the cause, of the foundation. (35, translation modified [F54])[14]

Since Marion gives a merely descriptive presentation in which he explicitly and fully endorses Heidegger's thought on this question, I shall not develop it here.[15]

The third step in Marion's strategy takes the form of a sudden reversal of his endorsement of Heidegger's thought, now *itself* criticized as metaphysical and thus idolatrous (hence the "second idolatry" suggested by the title of the chapter, "Double Idolatry").[16] The crux of the argument is that because later

Heidegger means to maintain an awareness of the ontological difference and thus to avoid the former confusions of onto-theology, being remains the transcendental horizon on which all the entities that show up are constituted as ontic. Consequently, the divine can appear only within our understanding of being, and therefore finds itself reduced to a mere phenomenon. Marion finds supporting evidence in the following quotation from Heidegger:

> Only from the truth of Being can the essence of the holy be thought. Only from the essence of the holy is the essence of the divinity to be thought. Only in the light of the essence of the divinity can it be thought or said what the word "God" is to name. (*Without* 39–40, translation modified [F61])[17]

This necessity for the sacred (and more generally, for anything, the sacred itself being identified by Marion as a particular class of phenomena, the "most protected of beings") (40 [F63]) to be disclosed on the background of being is the core of the ontological difference. As a result, Heidegger would, in his very attempt to preserve the latter, repeat the idolatrous mistake of metaphysics (although not in a foundational sense, since he does not think God as a *causa sui*) by reducing God to an ontic entity, fully captured within the space of its disclosure.

Consequently, the final element in Marion's attack is—unsurprisingly, given the anthropocentric structure of the idol—the claim that ultimately, being itself is made dependent by Heidegger on *Dasein's* disclosive abilities: "*Phenomenologically, the anteriority of Being can be developed and justified only by the anteriority of the analytic of Dasein. Therefore, one must admit the absolute phenomenological anteriority of Dasein*" (42, translation modified, my italics [F66]). In the third chapter, Marion builds on the rapprochement established by John Caputo between Heidegger and Thomas Aquinas, and reads the priority given by the latter to being (*ens*) over the Good in the naming of God as symptomatic of this reduction of the divine to the limits of human understanding (and therefore of the idolatrous character of any philosophical conceptualization of the divine) (77–83 [F119–124]): "The *ens* appears first, at least on condition that one takes the point of view of human understanding; the primacy of the *ens* depends on the primacy of a conception of the understanding and of the mind of man" (80 [F119]).[18] Hence Marion's general conclusion, which ties together the themes of disclosure and anthropocentrism in his criticism of Heidegger: "Any access to anything like 'God,' precisely because of the aiming-at of Being as such,[19] will have to determine Him in advance as a being" (43, translation modified [F68]).[20]

Once the ontological primacy of being over God has been exposed as a hidden case of idolatry—Heidegger's own unthought—it must be discarded in favor of the other mode of approach of the divine, the icon. Consequently, the final part of "Double Idolatry" and much of the rest of the book are devoted to fleshing out Marion's own solution to the problem of the paradoxical manifestation of God, to which I shall now turn briefly. In order to be consistent,

Marion's own approach must avoid the joint pitfalls of conceptualization and anthropomorphism: given the ties of both to the ontological difference, the only way out consists in "thinking outside of the ontological difference" (45 [F71]). Thus,

> By definition and decision, God, if he must be thought, can meet no theo-retical space to his measure, because his measure exerts itself in our eyes as excess [*démesure*]. The ontological difference itself, and hence also Being, become too limited . . . to pretend to offer the dimension, still less the "divine abode" where God would become thinkable. (ibid.)

Marion is very aware of the highly paradoxical nature of his endeavor[21] (since after all, one can think only from within an understanding of being), but reads this very paradox as a sign of adequation between his approach and its impossi-ble object: "But precisely, to be no longer able to think, when it is a question of God, indicates neither absurdity nor impropriety, as soon as God himself, in order to be thought, must be thought of as . . . that which surpasses, detours, and distracts all thought, even nonrepresentational" (ibid.).

Thinking outside of the ontological difference thus means inverting the priority of being over God: the crux of Marion's solution consists in a reversal in which the disclosed itself (God) must open up the space of its disclosure, a space therefore incommensurable to any human faculties. Our subsequent, radical impossibility of thinking God (symbolized, in an ironic reference to Heidegger, by the crossing of his name, G⨯d),[22] is thus read by Marion as a testimony to the iconic character of the relation thus established between him and man, a relation in which the centrality of an ontologically disclosive *Dasein* is displaced by the idea of a self-donation of the divine (hence Marion's anti-Heideggerian reinterpretation of the "gift" in chapter 3 of *Without*, "The Crossing of Being") (100–106 [F151–54]).[23] Finally, since thought and un-derstanding are, by definition, unsuited for relating to God (because they work through conceptualization), Marion puts a strong emphasis on love.[24] For him, the characteristics of love are symmetrically opposite to those of human understanding: love presupposes an unbridgeable distance between the lover and the loved one (as opposed to the idolatrous adequation between the space opened up by our faculties and the disclosed phenomenon). Moreover, it does not require that the beloved be understood: just like God himself (not surpris-ingly, since love comes from God), love is beyond being (as it is beyond intelligibility) and thus can name both the way in which God discloses himself to us and the manner in which we can reciprocate his gift. In Marion's iconic solution, the meaning of phenomenological disclosure is reversed, from an (over) determination of the object by the disclosive entity (expressed, accord-ing to him, by the structure of the idol) to an (equally over-determined, as we shall see) primacy of the disclosed over a suitably humbled *Dasein*: disclosure becomes absolute in that it transcends even the conditions of its own donation (47–49 [F73–75]).[25] Consequently,

> The second idolatry can be surpassed only in letting God be thought start-
> ing from his sole and pure demand. Such a demand goes beyond the limit
> of a concept—even that of metaphysics in its onto-the-ology—but also the
> limit of every condition whatsoever—even that of Being conceived in on-
> tological difference (48–49 [F75])

But is that really the case? Can we equate, as Marion does unabashedly, the necessity for phenomena to be disclosed against the background of our understanding of being with the idea that *Dasein* is the basis of all disclosure, and moreover that everything thus disclosed would be *fully* intelligible? For Heidegger, are the conditions of possibility of phenomenality so transparent that being is a mere "screen" on which everything becomes visible? I shall first develop a criticism of Marion's reconstruction of Heidegger before turning to my objections to his own solution.

Perhaps the first thing to note is that Marion does not offer much in terms of an *argument* against Heidegger (nor, actually, in favor of his own position). The necessity for anything to be disclosed within the horizon of being is dogmatically denounced as a dogmatic postulate, through a series of heavy rhetorical questions (see, for example, 44, 62, and 70). However, as much as he rejects Heidegger's interpretation as arbitrary (a "decision"), Marion does not explain to us why anything could (or should) show up without having our understanding of Being as its horizon of intelligibility.[26] The fact is that Hei-degger has some very good reasons for thinking so, which are grounded in his definition of being-in-the-world. But Marion cannot see them because he makes three fundamental mistakes in his exegesis. The first is that he reads Heidegger from a Husserlian point of view, and thus from a perspective which is not only extrinsic but also contrary to the substance of Heidegger's analyses. The second, which follows directly from the first, is that he makes our under-standing of being dependent on *Dasein*. The third is that, because he ignores the many Heideggerian attempts to deal with the problem of the potential closure of the hermeneutic circle, Marion unduly narrows down Heidegger's conception of phenomenality and commits Heidegger to a claim that he never made, namely that being disclosed means being *completely* intelligible, or again that nothing is ever withdrawn in the movement of disclosure. Com-bined in various ways, these three mistakes form the background of Marion's interpretation, such as in the following passage:

> For Heidegger a "God" other than the *causa sui* can and even must be
> envisaged; but to envisage, if the term is to have a phenomenological mean-
> ing, implies an aiming-at, and hence an aiming-at of Dasein. This aiming-
> at . . . must be understood on the basis of Dasein as such, as the being in
> which its being, or rather Being itself, is an issue. Consequently, the "more
> divine god" can be envisaged only within the limits of an aiming-at that
> determines it in advance as a being. (69, translation modified [F105])

Intentionality would be *Dasein's* way of relating to phenomena (hence Marion's insistence on "aiming"), and thus the ground of Heidegger's definition of being. Correlatively, disclosure would be fully transparent (hence the determination of God as a being by *Dasein's* intentional attitude).

That Marion has a Husserlian reading of Heidegger is very clear in the way he focuses on intentionality throughout *God Without Being*.[27] This focus is symbolically expressed, in the opening pages of the book, by the recurrence of the metaphors of the gaze and of representation in his analysis of the idol:

> The gaze makes the idol, not the idol the gaze—which means that *the idol with its visibility fills the intention of the gaze*, which wants nothing other than to see. The gaze precedes the idol because an aiming-at precedes and gives rise to that at which it aims. The first intention aims at the divine and the gaze strains itself to see the divine, to see it by taking it up into the field of the gazeable. (10–11, translation modified, my italics [F19])[28]

Significantly, the same paradigm also governs Marion's analysis of the *icon*: "The icon summons the gaze to surpass itself by never freezing on a visible, since the visible only presents itself here in view of the invisible" (18 [F29]). Since neither idol nor icon is an entity, but an antagonistic mode of disclosure which between the two encompass the whole of phenomenality (and even its beyond, as the idol is identified with ontological disclosure, and the icon with divine donation), it follows from this original characterization that for Marion, any form of disclosure is grounded, positively or negatively, in our ability to see and represent things—where vision stands as an explicit metaphor for intentionality. Consequently, Marion identifies intentionality as the way *Dasein* relates to the divine,[29] but also, more worryingly, as the defining characteristic of being-in-the-world: thus, *"no term can appear unless aimed at and seen by [Dasein]. Dasein precedes the question of 'God' in the very way that Being determines in advance . . . the divine, the holy, 'God,' his life and his death"* (43, my italics [F68]). As *Dasein's* intentional aiming is the source of all disclosure, our very understanding of being ends up depending on intentionality too: it becomes an ideal horizon, solipsistically and internally generated by the very structure of *Dasein's* aiming. From this basis, Marion argues that even the texts published after the *Kehre* should be read in the light of fundamental ontology thus (mis)reconstructed: "The later isolated anteriority of *Sein* is secured concretely by Dasein itself; phenomenologically, the anteriority of Being can be developed and justified only by the anteriority of the analytic of Dasein" (*Without* 42, translation modified [F66]).[30] Hence Marion's accusations of idolatry and anthropocentrism against Heidegger.

However, two points are worth making here: the first is that Marion reads fundamental ontology from the very perspective that Heidegger himself wanted to overcome in *Being and Time* and more explicitly in *The History of the Concept of Time*[31]—namely, the perspective of the Platonic-Cartesian pri-

macy of intuition (in its etymological sense, in other words, as insight (*in-tueri*)
which culminates in the Husserlian conception of intentionality as our primary mode of relating to phenomena. But Heidegger is very clear that "as
ontic transcendence, intentionality is itself only possible on the basis of originary transcendence, on the basis of Being-in-the-world. This primary transcendence makes possible every intentional relation to beings. . . . The relation is
based on a preliminary understanding of the being of beings" (*Logic* 135).[32]

Marion's Husserlian picture of both idol and icon should thus be reversed:
instead of projecting a horizon of visibility by means of its directedness, the
human gaze can aim at its objects only on the background of Dasein's having
a pre-comprehension of Being. Moreover, this "preliminary understanding"
itself is not theoretical, nor even thematic. Thus, "we must keep in mind
that knowing is grounded beforehand in a being-already-alongside-the-world,
which is essentially constitutive for Dasein's being" (Heidegger, *Being and
Time* 88). As initially shown by Hubert Dreyfus and developed by many others,[33] this being-already-alongside-the-world is grounded in our practical "dealings" with the world, in other words, our coping skills, not intentionality (95).
"Being-in-the-world . . . amounts to a non-thematic, circumspective absorp-
tion in references or assignments constitutive for the availableness of an equip-
mental whole" (107).

Moreover, the primacy unduly given to intentionality by Marion leads
him to misunderstand the nature of intelligibility itself: as we have seen,
for him intelligibility is the correlate of full visibility and, by metonymy, of
conceptualization: "The concept consigns to a sign what at first the mind
grasps with it (*concipere, capere*)" (*Without* 16 [F28]). Consequently, intelligibility is from the start restricted by the scope of our mental abilities: "Such
a grasp is measured . . . by the scope of a *capacitas*, which can fix the divine in a
specific concept only at the moment when a conception of the divine fills it,
hence appeases, stops, and freezes it" (ibid.).

But for Heidegger, intelligibility is not theoretical, not primarily conceptual.[34] It is grounded in state of mind (*Befindlichkeit*) and understanding
(*Verstehen*), neither of which is a detached mental activity. On the contrary, "as
a disclosure, understanding always pertains to the whole basic state of Being-in-
the-world" (*Being and Time* 184), which, as we have seen, is best apprehended
from our practical dealings with the world. Heidegger makes this point specifically against Husserl (although the latter is not named) in the following passage:

> By showing how all sight is grounded primarily in understanding . . . we
> have deprived pure intuition of its priority, which corresponds noetically to
> the priority of the present-at-hand in traditional ontology. Intuition and
> thinking are both derivative of understanding, and already rather remote
> ones. (187)

Thus in making being-in-the-world dependent on intentionality, Marion is
attributing to Heidegger a position exactly symmetrical to the one he really

held. Given that Marion starts with a truncated conception of phenomenal experience, it is hardly surprising that he should end up with a criticism of Heidegger's fundamental ontology as idolatrous, since idolatry (as adequation between the subject's directedness at something and its noematic fulfillment) is the very structure of intentionality itself.[35]

The second point bears on Marion's accusation of anthropocentrism. As Heidegger made his position very clear on this question,[36] I shall go directly to the third issue, which pertains to the relationship between disclosure and intelligibility. As we have seen, Marion's interpretation leaps from the necessity for the divine to appear within an understanding of being—a necessity acknowledged by Heidegger himself because, by definition (see above), as being-in-the-world entities we must have an understanding of being, an understanding that is the background of phenomenological disclosure—to the conclusion that the God thus disclosed would have to be a fully visible/intelligible entity.[37] "In short, 'God' first becomes visible as a being only, because he thus fills . . . and reflexively refers to itself an aiming that bears first and decidedly on Being" (*Without* 44 [F69]).[38] This jump itself comes from the anthropocentric definition of the idol as that which "does not admit any invisibility" (13 [F23]). However, there are many points to be made here. The first is that, as we have seen in the discussion of intentionality, for Heidegger being intelligible does not necessarily mean being theoretically understood. In Marion's terms, being visible does not mean being *integrally* visible. That phenomena should make sense to us in the very movement of their disclosure does not require that we fully understand their nature as present-at-hand entities, nor even that we conceptualize them. Thus in *Being and Time* the famous hammer makes sense to the carpenter who is using it without his having an awareness, let alone a concept, of the tool as an object. Not surprisingly given his Husserlian background, Marion unduly generalizes an analysis that would be, at best, more suited to a certain class of phenomena—namely, those that are intentionally disclosed as present-at-hand. I say "at best" because even in the latter case, entities can be disclosed as present-at-hand without being fully understood. In fact, one may even argue that for Heidegger *nothing* is ever disclosed as fully understood, in other words, understood right down to the conditions of its constitution. Even in *Being and Time*, where disclosure is most focused on *Dasein's* existential characteristics, the conditions of disclosure (our understanding of being) are never so transparent to us that being would be a mere screen on which phenomena would be projected. Again, this assumption is due to Marion's Husserlian reading of Heidegger. Only from this perspective could one, by describing exhaustively the structure of human intentionality, infer a full characterization both of the noema and of the horizon of meanings that they entail. But Heidegger's (explicitly anti-Husserlian) insistence on the hermeneutic circle as one in which we are always already existentially caught, without any clear starting point, precludes such a possibility: "When something in within-the-world is encountered as such, the thing in question already has an involvement which is disclosed in our understanding of the world, and this involvement is one which gets laid out by the interpretation" (*Being and Time* 190–191). Thus we can choose to tread the circle in a methodic way, and thereby deepen our comprehension of it, but there is no way in which our situation within it could be fully grasped. We move within an understanding of being that does not depend on us, and that we cannot completely clarify—if only because the clarifying activity itself modifies the understanding of being that it works on.[39]

Moreover—but this is the other side of the same coin—as our horizon of intelligibility, being may be presupposed by all our practices, but it is not given with them; because it is an open totality of cross-referenced relationships, by definition significance cannot be fully grasped by *Dasein*. Things have meaning for us, but what makes them *be* is always mysterious for us, even from the perspective closest to the one Marion describes, the *Dasein*-based forms of disclosure discussed in *Being and Time*. Thus, for Heidegger our understanding of being may be transcendental (in the sense that it is linked to human transcendence and determines the conditions under which things are intelligible to us), but it is not so in a Kantian or Husserlian sense. Heidegger's own version of the transcendental is a receding one, in which the conditions of human intelligibility structurally withdraw from the field they open.[40] Therefore, far from encapsulating Heidegger's definition of being, idolatrous disclosure never happens at all in the world that he describes. This is because, for the reasons just given, we are never in a situation in which the things disclosed would be integrally dependent on our aiming at them, and could be made fully intelligible, right down to the conditions of their constitution, by an analysis of our intentional attitudes. On the contrary, because of the very structure of the ontological difference, intelligibility and unintelligibility are tied together from the start: entities can be intelligible, be it partially or fully, only by being disclosed on the background of an understanding of being that itself constitutionally withdraws from our horizon of intelligibility. Consequently, Marion's diagnosis might just as well be reversed: far from being an idolatrous thinker, Heidegger could be cast as one of the staunchest opponents of idolatry, since for him the conditions of intelligibility can never be captured by the space that they open.

One may object that this does not address Marion's strongest point, that disclosure on the basis of our understanding of being would reduce God to an ontic being: even not fully understood, God would still "*have to be,* as a being manifested by Being, a being that manifests itself according to Being" (*Without* 70, translation modified [F106]). However, this presupposes that for Heidegger the only possible focus of disclosure would be entities. Hence Marion's implicit equation: to manifest oneself = to be a being. This may be true enough from the perspective of fundamental ontology, which still focuses on *Dasein* in order to understand disclosure. In *Being and Time*, *Dasein* can only disclose entities, either as ready-to-hand (equipment), as present-at-hand (objects), or as existing on the same mode as itself (other *Dasein*). If this were Heidegger's only and final position, then Marion would be right in claiming that the dependence of God's manifestation on our understanding of being would reduce him to an entity—although, as we have just seen, not a fully intelligible one because of the irreducible opacity of our comprehension of being. Onto-theology would be the radicalization of a structural necessity of human experience, namely, that everything (including God) should be disclosed as ontic. However, it is not the case that for Heidegger everything that can be disclosed has to be disclosed as an entity. In other words, it is not the case that disclosure is limited to a positive phenomenal content. This may be true in the case of the above-mentioned forms of disclosure, but much of Heidegger's later work was aimed at showing that there are other, non-*Dasein*-based forms of disclosure, in which what comes to the fore is neither an entity, nor fully intelligible. Indeed, his shift away from humanism was in good part motivated by his growing awareness of the danger of limiting disclosure to its *Dasein*-based forms. But because Marion minimizes the importance of this move so much as to negate it, he cannot see its consequences and therefore remains stuck with (his misrepresentation of) Heidegger's former model of disclosure. For lack of space, I will make only a few quick suggestions regarding later Heidegger's strategy before turning to my internal criticism of Marion.

"The Origin of the Work of Art" establishes that the kind of disclosure performed by artworks is such that, far from showing phenomena only, it opens up a space of truth (in the sense of *aletheia*—ontological disclosure, not ontic correspondence) in which both earth and world (neither of which are ontic) can come to the fore. Moreover, in this space the earth is brought forward as what fundamentally resists intelligibility, and such a resistance is deemed valuable, even essential, by Heidegger. Finally, in his analysis of the artwork Heidegger focuses for the first time on the *relationship* between intelligibility and what resists it. Indeed, what the artwork discloses is not only earth and world as ontological features, but mostly their "strife" (174)—in other words, the prolonged tension characteristic of the relationship between the horizon of phenomenality and what resists it: "In setting up a world and setting forth the earth, the work is an instigating of this strife . . . so that the strife remains a strife" (175). The relationship between the hermeneutic circle and its outside, instead of being envisioned only negatively (the latter being the mere limit of the former), and in passing (as fundamental ontology was focused on a description of the ontological lineaments of being-in-the-world), acquires a new positivity in the sense that it becomes perceptible (although not theoretically understood) in the artwork. The borderline between intelligibility and what falls outside of it now appears as a moving, dynamic zone, in which each of the opponents (world and earth) finds a richer definition of itself. Since later Heidegger considerably deepens his understanding of phenomenality, both by uncovering the possibility of a disclosure of the ontological elements that structure human experience,[41] and by rethinking the status and the value of the limits of the hermeneutic circle, Marion is wrong in assimilating disclosure with ontic, *Dasein*-based disclosure. Certain entities—although, granted, not the ones described in *Being and Time*—have the ability to perform a different kind of disclosure in which what shows up (the world, the earth, the Fourfold) is not dependent on *Dasein* for its constitution, and moreover shows up *as such*—in other words, in its fundamental irreducibility to human understanding. Such a disclosure does not close the hermeneutic circle upon itself: it shows *that the circle was never truly closed in the first place*—not even in *Being and Time*, since the conditions of phenomenal intelligibility are never transparent to us. Therefore, in Marion's own terms, the paradigm best suited to think disclosure in Heidegger's thought ends up being, ironically enough, the icon, not the idol.

Moreover, although Marion seems unaware of it, later Heidegger's own concern is to ensure that this fundamental openness is not reduced by our current understanding of being, in other words, that the struggle between earth and world can be preserved, that the earth itself does not vanish as what resists intelligibility, that the gods do not desert the mortals. As his further analyses of *Gestell* and of technology show him that this is a matter of urgency, Heidegger develops (for example in *What Is Called Thinking?*) new strategies that I will only suggest here. Among these is the redefinition of thought as a non-representational, non-objectifying way of relating to things, an alternative to conceptualization that could have addressed Marion's legitimate queries about the reductive character of human intelligibility. Thought—as opposed to philosophy, which by definition tries to understand its objects—becomes, per se, a way to deny the usual priority given to intelligibility, and thus to preserve, in the very activity of thinking, the resistance of what we think to thought itself. Another element in the same strategy is the bringing to the fore of the constitutive link between thought and *Stimmung* (especially such *Stimmungen* as love and gratitude, as suggested by the etymology *denken/danken*).[42] This emphasis on the centrality of moods and, more generally, of human affectivity in thinking is essential because it offers a remedy to the grasping character of detached, conceptual reasoning. This leads Heidegger to define receptivity as the kind of *Befindlichkeit* specific to thought. Receptivity is not passivity, since it is coextensive to thinking, and for Heidegger thinking is perhaps the hardest of all tasks—as he constantly repeats, dwelling with a question and thus letting it develop, both in accordance with itself and in its resistance against our thinking process. Thinking is much more difficult than solving a question too quickly. But receptivity is not activity either, as our nihilistic, technological understanding of being takes it, an understanding in which activity has taken the threatening aspect of an intellectual *Gestell* which, by seeking immediate and complete intelligibility, is bound to reduce its object to what it can understand of it, and thus close the circle as soon as it has opened it. Although Marion is prevented by his own assumptions from realizing it, much of Heidegger's later work is in fact devoted to finding in thought and its accompanying *Stimmungen* an *analogon* to the formerly identified artistic mode of disclosure, a mode in which the limits of intelligibility themselves become visible in the thinking itself.

Thus in making Heidegger's understanding of Being dependent on *Dasein*, in reading being-in-the-world as based on intentionality, and in assuming that all forms of disclosure are transparent and ontic, Marion is misconstruing Heidegger to the point of almost devoiding his own criticism of any validity. In conclusion, I would like to examine whether Marion does better on his own terms. Marion presents the gist of Heidegger's own thoughts on the question (although with polemical intentions) in the following quotation from the Zürich Seminar:

> I believe that Being can never be thought of as the ground and essence of God, but that nevertheless the experience of God and of his manifestedness, to the extent that the latter can indeed meet man, flashes in the dimension of Being, which in no way signifies that Being might be regarded as a possible predicate for God. (*Without* 208 [F63])

However, Heidegger is being very consistent here in distinguishing implicitly between two levels, that of existence on the one hand, and of (phenomenal) manifestation, "manifestedness," on the other hand. From the perspective of existence, there is no dependence whatsoever between God and being. Being is neither the ground (in the sense of the principle of sufficient reason[43]) nor the essence of God (a set of ontological determinations that would be actualized in existence). But from the perspective of his manifestation to humanity, God *is* dependent on being in the sense that for us, *any* phenomenal manifestation must occur within the horizon of being, although as we have seen it does not follow that God should be fully understood within it, nor that he should be an entity. Thus, for us the "experience of God" must "flash in the dimension of Being," but, conversely, its flashing brightness stands as the symbol of the impossibility for our understanding of being to encompass the divine. Thus, Heidegger remains faithful to the end to his original reinterpretation of transcendental idealism: just as the thing-in-itself is not dependent for its existence, but only for its phenomenal manifestation, on transcendental determination, in the same way, God's existence is per se separate from our understanding of being, which becomes relevant to him only from the phenomenal perspective of his relationship to *Dasein*. Just as in the case of the "real" considered per se, *is* is not a suitable predicate.

But Marion's answer to the same problem, although it starts from similar premises, does not display the same consistency:

> If, by an anhypothetical hypothesis that we admit absolutely, the question of Being is determined only in relation to itself, namely, according to the claim that Being exerts over *Dasein* and that defines from the start transcendentally every world that will be constituted as such, must one not infer *also, according to the same rigor,* that that which, by hypothesis, does not

> belong to this world from the perspective of its existence and gives itself as such, does not refer/belong [*relever*] to Being? (*Without* 71, translation modified, italics Marion's [F107])

Marion's implicit syllogism can be decomposed in the following way:

> a) The question of being is only relevant from the perspective of the relationship between being and *Dasein*, and within this context determines the meaning of the world (as our understanding of being defines the conditions of phenomenal intelligibility).
> b) God does not belong to this world—Marion argues that it is the case from John's authority (John 18:36).
> Therefore, c) it should follow that the question of being, which is relevant only to *Dasein* and the world, does not apply to God: God is beyond being.

However, even if one were to grant the unverifiable premise entailed by b) (God's existence as testified by John), the syllogism would still be faulty for at least two reasons. The first one is that, contrary to Heidegger, Marion confuses conditions of existence and conditions of phenomenal manifestation. Indeed, the claim that God "does not belong to this world" refers to God's logical and ontological anteriority over the world (as its Creator), and therefore to the sheer fact of God's eternal existence, which of course is not dependent on the human world (quite to the contrary). Therefore, from the standpoint of existence (assuming that God exists), Marion is quite right to say that the question of being does not apply to God—Heidegger himself did not say anything different in the Zürich seminar. But as soon as God is revealed to us ("*given* as such"), then the question of being becomes relevant—although only from the perspective of phenomenal manifestation—because in *Dasein's* case, all forms of disclosure presuppose by definition our having an understanding of being. In spite of Marion's claim to the contrary ("*according to the same rigor*"—his italics), the inference from unconditioned existence to unconditioned manifestation does not work, quite simply because the two levels are incommensurable to each other.

The second fault in Marion's solution (which follows from the first) is therefore that the notion of an unconditioned manifestation contradicts the phenomenological premises that Marion himself repeatedly endorses.[44] Marion is explicit that his aim is to "think God without any conditions, not even that of Being, hence to think God without pretending to inscribe him or to describe him as a being" (*Without* 45 [F70]) or, again, to think "the excess of an absolute donation—absolute" (48, translation modified [F75]). However, the first aim, "to think God without any condition," is a phenomenological impossibility. As we have seen, thought can at best reflect on its own conditions and try to bring their limits to the fore in the very operation of thinking, and as result disclose things on a mode analogically similar to that of the artwork, a direction that was explored by Heidegger in *What Is Called Thinking?* But—as indicated by the paradoxical need for Marion himself to express in human words his views about God's fundamental incommensurability to human thought—unconditioned thinking, like unconditioned experience, is simply self-contradictory. As Marion himself acknowledges,[45] "unthinkability" remains a (negative) predicate of thought. In fact, the core of the problem is that Marion is implicitly reverting to a metaphysical understanding of transcendence (as that which is "definitively other"),[46] the disclosure of which would bypass the conditions defined by being-in-the-world as phenomenological transcendence. The metaphysical or theological tradition had a name for such an absolute disclosure: Revelation. From the perspective of this tradition, absolute disclosure is not contradictory. Since, prior to the Copernican turn, experience was not seen as dependent on the transcendental subject for its constitution, the notion of a self-presentation or absolute donation of the divine was not only consistent, but even central to the very definition of human understanding, which in turn was thought of as limited in its powers and fundamentally dependent on God's light.[47] Thus in Marion's dramatic shift from disclosure to divine Revelation (*Without* 46–47 [F71–72]), the Copernican inheritance undergoes in fact an additional and polemical revolution which, ironically, brings it back to its precritical starting point. The divine must shine directly through human experience and transform its very conditions of possibility. In other words, the thing-in-itself must be understood as unconditionally self-disclosive, a possibility of course rejected from the start by the first *Critique*. Perhaps most idolatrous of all, Marion therefore endows human beings with one of the attributes that Kant himself had reserved to God, an *intuitus originarius*. Not surprisingly, Marion's position ends up as unsustainable because he tries to revert to a precritical conception of human experience while endorsing at the same time its post-Copernican, phenomenological definition.[48]

Thus, the fundamental claims of *God Without Being* are untenable because they rest on a misinterpretation of fundamental ontology which, combined with a disregard for later Heidegger's many attempts to deal with the issues raised, leads Marion to misunderstand the Heideggerian conception of the conditions of phenomenality, and thus to present solutions strangely akin to Heidegger's own. Marion's definition of the idol as a full, *Dasein*-based mode of disclosure, rather than encompassing Heidegger's ultimate rethinking of the ontological difference, ends up being inapplicable to his thought from the start. Conversely, the iconic structure, originally presented as a foil against Heidegger, turns out to be a better—although not fully adequate—way of describing the latter's reworking of the modalities of phenomenological disclosure. If anything, the polarity of Marion's seminal distinction should thus be ironically reversed. But more fundamentally, the very relevance of this distinction to Heidegger appears doubtful, as it implicitly rests on a Husserlian understanding of intentionality as the primary condition of possibility of disclosure.

Nonetheless, although it does not qualify as the devastating criticism of

Heidegger that it is meant to be, Marion's approach is interesting in that it rightly brings to the fore a problem central both to Heidegger and to phenomenology: that of the limits of phenomenological disclosure and of the primacy of intelligibility in understanding disclosure itself. As we have seen, Marion's own answer is unacceptable because it entails a conflation between two distinct dimensions, that of existence and that of phenomenal manifestation. Thus, Marion argued from God's autonomous existence to the possibility of an absolute donation of the divine, which would transcend the very conditions of phenomenality (being itself). In doing so, he both asserted and tried to circumvent the conditions of phenomenality by leaping outside of them, a self-contradictory and impossible attempt. But this failure is valuable in that it shows us that the danger of hermeneutic closure cannot be dealt with by means of a sheer denial of the hermeneutic circle itself. Just as the way out of our technological understanding of being, if it exists, does not lie outside of technicity but in technicity itself, the remedy to the potentially anthropocentric and nihilistic character of human understanding does not reside in a rejection of its limitations. If finitude is to be dealt with, it must be from the inside. Contrary to Marion, Heidegger acknowledged this necessity and struggled with it in his later work, by trying to find alternative ways of relating to the circle itself, and by exploring alternative modes of disclosure. Whether these ways are successful or not, I cannot discuss within the limits of this paper. However, we can safely assume that whatever the answer is, it won't be so for the reasons given by Marion in *God Without Being*.

NOTES

1. See, for example, Janicaud, *Le tournant théologique, La philosophie en Europe*, and *La phénoménologie éclatée*. Publication of the first book generated a heated debate, which itself gave rise to many publications, among them Courtine, *Phénoménologie et Théologie* (which includes papers by Marion, Henry, Ricoeur, and Chrétien).

2. "We admit therefore, without arguing or even explaining it here, the radical anteriority of ontological difference as that through which and as which the *Geschick* of Being deploys beings, in a retreat that nevertheless saves a withdrawn proximity. We also admit that the ontological difference is operative in metaphysical thought only in the forgetful figure of a thought of Being (a thought summoned to and by Being) that, each time, keeps the ontological difference unthought as such" (*Without* 33–34 [F52]). (References to the original French will follow the English edition citations between brackets and preceded by an "F").

3. The identification between *Dasein* and transcendence is explicitly made by Heidegger in *The Essence of Reasons*.

4. "We therefore posit that here again, a second time, and beyond the idolatry specific to metaphysics, there functions another idolatry, specific to the thought of Being as such. This affirmation, as blunt as it may seem, derives nevertheless directly from the indisputable and essential anteriority of the ontological question over the so-called 'ontic' question of 'God.' This anteriority suffices to establish idolatry" (*Without* 41, translation modified [F65]).

5. "The gift does not have first to be, but to pour out in an abandon that, alone, causes it to be; God saves the gift in giving it before being" (*Without* 3; [F12]).

6. Marion plays on the ambivalence of the French "absolu," which, apart from "absolute," also means (etymologically, *ab-solvere*) freed from all ties. Marion goes on to give examples of "saturated phenomena," such as "pure historical events" and, significantly, "revelation phenomena" (215–16 [F126–28]).

7. Thus, one must "think God without any conditions, not even that of Being, hence to think God without pretending to inscribe him or to describe him as a being" (*Without* 45 [F70]).

8. In *God Without Being*, Marion already defines God as that which "crosses out our thought because he saturates it" ("Dieu rature notre pensée parce qu'il la sature" (46 [F72]). The metaphor of saturation recurs many times in the same pages, for example, "[God's] unthinkableness saturates our thought—right from the beginning, and forever" (46 [F73]).

9. Thus he joins a more general debate, as this question is also, for example, Michel Henry's *L'essence de la manifestation*; it is also, although in a different way, the driving force behind Levinas's reflection on the other as what transcends intelligibility. I shall return to this point in my conclusion.

10. Compare what Heidegger says: "The 'universality' of 'Being' is not that of a *class* or a *genus*. The term 'Being' does not define that realm of entities which is uppermost when these are articulated conceptually according to genus and species" (*Being and Time* 22).

11. See also 8 [F16]: "The icon and the idol determine two manners of being for beings, not two classes of beings."

12. Very significantly, Marion's analysis of these two modes of disclosure is focused on notions which were central to Husserl's phenomenology but explicitly criticized by Heidegger, such as intentionality or representation. I shall come back to this in order to question the suitability of Marion's application of this distinction to Heidegger's thought.

13. See Marion's more detailed analyses at 30–33.

14. In a very Heideggerian manner, Marion reads the Nietzschean proclamation of the death of God as a mere continuation of metaphysics as the "new gods" depend on the "religious instinct" of the *Gottbildende*, and therefore are too aesthetically and conceptually determined by the will to power. "Ainsi, à une appréhension idolâtrique succède une autre appréhension idolâtrique: la manifestation du divin passe seulement d'une condition (morale) à une autre (*Wille Zur Macht*) sans que jamais le divin ne se libère comme tel" (*Sans l'être* 59; *Without* 36).

15. Compare: "We admit therefore, without arguing or even explaining it here, the radical anteriority of ontological difference as that through and as which the *Geschick* of Being deploys as beings, in a retreat that nevertheless saves a withdrawn proximity. We also admit that ontological difference is operative in metaphysical thought only in the forgetful figure of a thought of Being (thought summoned to and by Being) that, each time, keeps ontological difference unthought as such" (*Without* 33–34 [F53]).

16. This reversal is evoked for the first time as follows: "Does retroceding from metaphysics, assuming that the thought devoted to Being can do so, suffice to free God from idolatry—for does idolatry come to its end with the *causa sui* or, on the contrary, does the idolatry of the *causa sui* not refer, as a hint only, to another idolatry, more discrete, more pressing, and therefore all the more threatening?" (*Without* 37, translation modified [F58]).

17. The quote itself is taken from Heidegger, "Letter on Humanism." Marion himself paraphrases it a bit later as follows: "The truth on 'God' could never come but from where truth itself issues, namely from Being as such, from its constellation and its opening" (*Without* 41 [F65]).

18. One may argue, of course, that *ens* has very different meanings for Thomas and for Heidegger (as shown by Caputo himself). However, Marion does not hesitate to bring the two understandings extremely close together: "Tout se passe comme si la primauté de la question de l'Être (Heidegger) rencontrait, sans confusion certes et avec tout l'écart qui sépare une pensée qui rétrocède de la métaphysique d'une pensée qui y demeure, la primauté de l'*ens* sur tout autre nom divin (saint Thomas)" (*Sans l'être* 108; *Without* 72).

19. Which, for Marion, is itself dependent on *Dasein*; see the top of 68 [F102]. A serious mistake in his exegesis of Heidegger, to which I shall return shortly.

20. Compare: "Being offers in advance the screen on which any 'God' that would be constituted would be projected and would appear—since by definition, to be constituted signifies to be constituted as a being. To be constituted as being of/in Being, as one surrenders oneself as a prisoner [*se constitue prisonnier*—literally, the 'divine prisoner'] of Being?" (*Without* 70 [F105]).

21. "Indeed, to think outside of the ontological difference eventually condemns one to be no longer able to think at all" (*Without* 45 [F71]).

22. "The unthinkable taken as such is the concern of God himself, and characterizes him as the *aura* of his advent, the glory of his insistence, the brilliance of his retreat. The unthinkable determines God by the seal of his definitive indeterminateness for a created and finite thought" (*Without* 46 [F72]).

23. The gist of the analysis is that whereas for Heidegger the gift should be understood from its own structure (as unfolding in the Fourfold) and therefore is ultimately dependent on being and (given Marion's reduction of being to *Dasein*) on its receiver, in fact the true meaning of the gift resides in the giver. The gift cannot be understood as the self-presencing of being but presupposes an essential distance (between God and the creature) which itself cannot be bridged by the understanding (as this would immediately bring the giver within the horizon of being) but by love as "hyperbolic *agapê*."

24. "Double Idolatry" (*Without* 47–49 [F73–75]). See also "The Crossing of Being" (102–107 [F148–55])

25. *Without* 47–49 [F73–75], and more particularly the following: "In the case of love man cannot impose any condition, *even negative*, on the initiative of God. Thus no aim can any longer decide idolatrously on the possibility or impossibility of access to and from 'God' " (*Without* 48 [F74]). Note, again, the vocabulary of intentionality.

26. In "The Crossing of Being" (71–73 [F92–109], Marion offers a reading of Heidegger's text "Phenomenology and Theology" in which theology appears as an "ontic science of faith." However, on top of the fact that this is an early text, the determination of theology as an ontic discipline does not commit Heidegger himself to the view that God is a being. It does not address either the problem of the meaning of disclosure itself.

27. This is also hardly surprising as, like the bulk of Marion's writings on phenomenology (for example, *Réduction et donation*, *La croisée du visible*, and *Étant donné*), "The Saturated Phenomenon" either bears on Husserl or is written from Husserlian premises.

28. This page and the next few (up to 24) are devoted to the primacy and centrality of the human gaze. The French *regard* recurs almost at every line. In the opening pages of "Double Idolatry," so does, significantly, the French *visée* (aiming at), the standard French translation of Husserl's "directedness."

29. "Each time, therefore, the idol indeed testifies to the divine, but each time the divine thought starting from its aiming-at, limited to a variable scope, by Dasein" (*Without* 28, translation modified [F43]).

30. See also the following: "In the texts examined above, the dependence of 'God' . . . on Being does not seem to have its origin in an ontically identifiable gaze; thus Heidegger would not satisfy one of the conditions of the idol. In fact, one should not forget, in reading the texts subsequent to the 'turn,' the (in fact *definitive*) accomplishment of earlier texts having to do with the analytic of Dasein and the fundamental essence of phenomenology" (*Without* 42 [F66]). Significantly, the defining characteristic of *Dasein* is, once more, its "gaze."

31. *Being and Time* itself mentions Husserl very seldom. However, Heidegger engages with transcendental phenomenology much more explicitly in the 1925 course (published as *The History of the Concept of Time*), and in *The Basic Problems of Phenomenology* (23–79).

32. See also *Basic Problems* 162: "It will turn out that intentionality is founded in Dasein's transcendence and is possible solely for this reason—that transcendence cannot conversely be explained in terms of intentionality." On the question of intentionality in Husserl and Heidegger, see (among others) Carr, and more specifically Hopkins. It can be argued that Heidegger himself is simplifying the Husserlian understanding of intentionality (see, for example, Keller, especially chapter 5).

33. See Dreyfus, *Commentary*, especially chapter 3 (46–53). See also Taylor, "Engaged Agency" and "What's Wrong with Foundationalism?"

34. "Discourse" (*Rede*) underlies language (*Sprache*) as an existential.

35. Hence, Marion's own subsequent dialogue with and criticism of Husserl in *Étant donné*. However, this text (1997) is posterior by almost twenty years to *God without Being*. ("Double Idolatry" was written in 1979, "The Crossing of Being" in 1980.)

36. However, although Marion *himself* uses the terms *Dasein* and *man* interchangeably throughout *God without Being*, they were never interchangeable for Heidegger, not from the start. Thus, in response to Husserl's attacks against fundamental ontology as a form of transcendental psychologism (made in his copy of *Being and Time*, cf. Diemer 19–21), Heidegger replied, "If the human being is only a human being *on the ground of the Dasein in him*, then the question concerning what is more original than a human being cannot be an anthropological one" (*Kant and the Problem*, §41). Moreover (as is well known) after the *Kehre* Heidegger himself tried explicitly to reduce the part formerly given to *Dasein* in *Being and Time*. "Letter on Humanism" expands on the displacement of "man" as the former object of philosophical inquiry by means of a further de-centering of *Dasein* itself: the *da-* of *Dasein*, the *Lichtung*, should be understood from being itself, not from *Dasein*. Thus, "Metaphysics closes itself to the simple essential fact that man essentially occurs only in his essence, where he is claimed by Being." Only from that claim "has he found that wherein his essence dwells. . . . Such standing in the clearing of Being I call the ek-sistence of man" ("Letter" 227–28). Conversely, *Dasein* is assigned a responsibility, which is to maintain a sense of the clearing—that is, to raise the question of being and to keep it open, but in doing so,

Dasein is only the "shepherd" (245), not the master, of being. To cast this in the terms of fundamental ontology, our understanding of being is presupposed and conveyed by our everyday practices, and we can to some extent try to bring its structure to the fore and thus become more aware of it (which is what Heidegger himself is doing in *Being and Time*), but we do not control it.

37. The symbolic identification between visibility and intelligibility is made by Marion's analysis of conceptualization itself as idolatrous. See above.

38. Significantly, our relation to being is, here again, one of aiming at.

39. An example of this would be the way in which Foucault's analysis of how the relationship between power and homosexuality has changed and is changing our current understanding of what it means to be "gay." See my paper, "Nietzsche and Foucault on Style."

40. In fact, Heidegger may be closer to Kant than it seems, at least according to Foucault's reading of the relationship between the first *Critique* and the *Anthropology*, in the sense that "man" comes to occupy this withdrawing spot. This structure is described in *The Order of Things* as the "return of the origin." Correlatively, the impossibility of accounting for the transcendental conditions of possibility of intelligibility may have some unexpected drawbacks (such as the impossibility of founding transcendental philosophy), but as they are not relevant to Marion's criticism of Heidegger, I shall leave this problem aside. See my paper, "Heidegger and Foucault."

41. Although I don't have time to develop this theme here, it is clear that the "thing," by revealing the "Fourfold"—that is, the ontological junction of the mortals, the sky, the earth, and the gods—performs a similar kind of disclosure to that of the artwork.

42. See *Thinking* (6–7, as well as 343, 135, 140–41, and 203).

43. See Heidegger, *The Principle of Reason*.

44. In the last extended quotation, Marion accepts the idea that Dasein's understanding of Being determines what it means to be a world, but also more generally. See also the passages quoted in the introduction to this paper.

45. "Concerning God, let us admit clearly that we can think him only under the figure of the unthinkable, but of an unthinkable that exceeds as much what we cannot think as what we can; for that which I may not think is still the concern of *my* thought, and hence to *me* remains thinkable" (*Without* 46 [F72]).

46. Thus, Marion questions the idea that "it [is] self-evident that the phenomenological enterprise of an analytic of Dasein did not admit, by its very reduction any exterior and definitively other instance" (71 [F107]).

47. For example, this is Augustine's position in the *Confessions*.

48. A similar criticism is formulated by Dominique Janicaud against Marion's reinterpretation of donation in *Étant donné*. See *La phénoménologie éclatée*: the postulate of "an 'absolutely unconditioned intuitive donation' cancels in one stroke the whole of the critical work, and reintroduces under the name of 'saturated phenomenon' . . . the noumenon!" (65).

WORKS CITED

Carr, David. *Interpreting Husserl: Critical and Comparative Studies*. Dordrecht: Martinus Nijhoff, 1987.

Courtine, Jean-François, ed. *Phénoménologie et Théologie*. Paris: Criterion, 1992.

Diemer, Alwin. *Edmund Husserl*. Maisenheim: Hain, 1965.

Dreyfus, Hubert. *Being-in-the-World: A Commentary on Heidegger's Being and Time, Division 1*. Cambridge: MIT Press, 1992.

Foucault, Michel. *The Order of Things: An Archaeology of the Human Sciences*. New York: Pantheon, 1971.

Han, Béatrice. "Heidegger and Foucault on Kant and Finitude." In Alan Milchman, ed., *Critical Encounters: Heidegger/Foucault*. Cambridge University Press, forthcoming.

——. "Nietzsche and Foucault on Style: the Limits of the Aesthetic Paradigm." In Endre Kiss and Uschi Nussbaumer-Benz, eds., *Nietzsche, Postmodernismus und was nach ihnen kommt*, 122–148. Dartford: Junghaus, 2000.

Heidegger, Martin. *The Basic Problems of Phenomenology*. Trans. Albert Hofstadter. Bloomington: Indiana University Press, 1982.

——. *Being and Time*. Trans. John Macquarrie and Edward Robinson. New York: Harper and Row, 1962.

——. *The Essence of Reasons*. Trans. Terrence Malick. Evanston, Ill.: Northwestern University Press, 1969.

——. *The History of the Concept of Time*. Trans. Theodore Kiesel. Bloomington: Indiana University Press: 1985.

——. *Kant and the Problem of Metaphysics*. Trans. James Churchill. Bloomington: Indiana University Press, 1962.

——. "Letter on Humanism." In M. Heidegger, *Basic Writings: From* Being and Time *(1927) to* The Task of Thinking *(1964)*. Ed. David Farrell Krell. 2nd rev. and exp. ed., 143–212. San Francisco: HarperSanFrancisco, 1993.

——. *The Metaphysical Foundations of Logic*. Trans. Michael Heim. Bloomington: Indiana University Press, 1984.

——. "The Origin of the Work of Art." In M. Heidegger, *Poetry Language Thought*, trans. Albert Hofstadter, 15–87. New York: Harper & Row, 1975.

——. *The Principle of Reason*. Trans. Reginald Lilly. Bloomington: Indiana University Press, 1991.

——. *What Is Called Thinking*. Introduction by J. Glenn Gray. New York: Harper & Row, 1972.

Henry, Michel. *L'Essence de la manifestation*. Paris: Presses Universitaires de France, 1980.

Hopkins, Burt. *Intentionality in Husserl and Heidegger: The Problem of Original Method and Phenomenon of Phenomenology*. Dordrecht: Kluwer, 1993.

Janicaud, Dominique. *La phénoménologie éclatée*. Paris: Editions de l'Éclat, 1998.

——. *La philosophie en Europe*. Paris: Gallimard, 1993.

——. *Le tournant théologique de la phénoménologie française*. Paris: Éditions de l'Éclat, 1991.

Keller, Pierre. *Husserl and Heidegger on Human Experience*. Cambridge: Cambridge University Press, 1999.

Marion, Jean-Luc. *La croisée du visible*. Paris: Presses Universitaires de France, 1996.

——. *Dieu sans l'Être*. Paris: Presses Universitaires de France, 1982. Translated as *God Without Being*. Trans. Thomas A. Carlson. Chicago: University of Chicago Press, 1991.

——. *Étant donné: Essai d'une phénoménologie de la donation*. Paris: Presses Universitaires de France, 1997.

——. "Le phénomène saturé." In Jean-Francois Courtine, ed., *Phénoménologie et Théologie*, 79–128. Paris: Criterion, 1992. Translated as "The Saturated Phenomenon," in Dominique Janicaud, Jean-François Courtine, Jean-Louis Chrétien, Jean-Luc Marion, Michel Henry, and Paul Ricoeur, *Phenomenology and the "Theological Turn": The French Debate*, trans. Bernard G. Prusak, Jeffrey L. Kosky, and Thomas A. Carlson, 176–216. New York: Fordham University Press, 2000.

——. *Réduction et donation, Recherches sur Husserl, Heidegger et la phénoménologie*. Paris: Presses universitaires de France, 1989. Translated as *Reduction and Givenness: Investigations of Husserl, Heidegger, and Phenomenology*. Trans. Thomas A. Carlson. Evanston: Northwestern University Press, 1998.

Taylor, Charles. "Engaged Agency and Background in Heidegger." In Charles Guignon, ed., *Cambridge Companion to Heidegger*, 317–336. Cambridge: Cambridge University Press, 1993.

——. "What's Wrong with Foundationalism? Knowledge, Agency, and the World." In Mark Wrathall and Jeff Malpas, eds., *Heidegger, Coping, and Cognitive Science: Essays in Honor of Hubert L. Dreyfus*, vol. 2, 115–134. Cambridge: MIT Press, 2000.

CONTRIBUTORS

JAMES E. FAULCONER is Professor of Philosophy at Brigham Young University and, with Mark Wrathall, editor of *Appropriating Heidegger* (2000). He is also the founding editor of *Epoché: A Journal for the History of Philosophy*.

BÉATRICE HAN is a Lecturer in Philosophy at the University of Essex (UK). A graduate of the Ecole Normale Supérieure, she is the author of *Foucault's Critical Project: Between the Transcendental and the Historical* (2002). She is currently working on a book entitled *Transcendence Without Religion*.

JEAN-LUC MARION is Professor of Philosophy at the University of Paris-Sorbonne (Paris IV), editor of the series "Epimethéeè" (Presses universitaires de France), Director of the "Centre d'Etudes Cartésiennes" (University of Paris-Sorbonne), and Visiting Professor (Department of Philosophy) at the University of Chicago. His works include several books on Descartes and early modern philosophy and *God Without Being* (1991), *Reduction and Givenness* (1999), *The Idol and Distance* (2001), *Prolegomena to Charity* (2002), and *Etant donné: essai d'une phénoménologie de la donation* (1997, 1998), translated as *Being Given* (forthcoming 2003).

PAUL MOYAERT studied philosophy in Louvain and in Paris. He teaches philosophical anthropology and ethics at the Catholic University of Louvain. He is a trained psychoanalyst and author of a book on the ethics of Jacques Lacan, *Ethiek en sublimatie* (1996); a book on neighborly love, the sense for symbols, and mystic love, *De mateloosheid of het Christendom* (1999); and a book on sublimation and idealization in psychoanalysis, *Begeren en vereren* (2002).

BEN VEDDER is professor of metaphysics and philosophy of religion at Nijmegen University (The Netherlands). He publishes in German and English on hermeneutics, metaphysics, and philosophy of religion. His recent publications include *Was ist Hermeneutik? Ein Weg von der Textdeutung zur Interpretation der Wirklichkeit* (2000).

Contributors

MEROLD WESTPHAL is professor of philosophy at Fordham University, and has published widely in nineteenth- and twentieth-century European philosophy, especially in relation to Christian faith. His recent published works include *Overcoming Onto-theology: Toward a Postmodern Christian Faith* (2001).

MARLÈNE ZARADER teaches philosophy at Université Paul-Valery (Montpelier). She is the author of *Heidegger et les Paroles de l'origine* (1986, 1990), which has been translated into Italian and Portuguese; and *La dette impensée. Heidegger et l'héritage hébraïque* (1990), which has been translated into Japanese, Italian, and Portuguese. An English translation of the second is forthcoming. Her latest book is *L'être et le neutre. A partir de Maurice Blanchot* (2001).

INDEX

Index

Index